EVALUATION PROGRAMS for SCHOOL BANDS and ORCHESTRAS

Russell A. Pizer

PARKER PUBLISHING COMPANY
West Nyack, New York 10995

© 1990 *by*

PARKER PUBLISHING COMPANY

West Nyack, New York

10 9 8 7 6 5 4 3 2 1

Library of Congress Cataloging-in-Publication Data

Pizer, Russell A.
    Evaluation programs for school bands and orchestras / Russell A.
Pizer.
        p.   cm.
    ISBN 0-13-292301-7
    1. Instrumental music—Instruction and study. 2. Musical
instruments—Instruction and study. 3. School music—Instruction
and study. 4. Orchestra—Instruction and study. 5. Bands (Music)—
Instruction and study. 6. Music—Examinations, questions, etc.
I. Title.
MT170.P58 1990
784′.97—dc20   89-48092
                                                         CIP
                                                         MN

ISBN 0-13-292301-7

PARKER PUBLISHING COMPANY
BUSINESS & PROFESSIONAL DIVISION
A division of Simon & Schuster
West Nyack, New York 10995

Printed in the United States of America

About the Author

Russell A. Pizer has taught instrumental music at all levels from fourth grade flutophone, to university conducting classes, to stage band at San Quentin Prison. He has also acted as a clinician and served as a music department chairman, guest conductor, adjudicator, guest lecturer, and recitalist.

He holds two degrees from the University of Michigan. While doing post-graduate study at the University of Michigan, he held a teaching fellowship and developed a unique manual for making long-lay oboe reeds which has been published by Jack Spratt Woodwind Shop.

Mr. Pizer has written extensively for *The Instrumentalist*. He has had a four-part series on competitions/festivals published in the *School Music News*. After he published a six-part series on New York State regulations governing music teaching in the schools, he developed a Government Relations Committee within the New York School Music Association.

Mr. Pizer is also the author of *Administering the Elementary Band, How to Improve the High School Band Sound,* and *Instrumental Music Evaluation Kit: Forms & Procedures for Assessing Student Performance,* all published by Parker Publishing Company.

170219

About This Book

Evaluation Programs for School Bands and Orchestras will help all music directors and music educators, grades 5–12, to do "on paper" evaluations of various aspects of their instrumental music programs. Although one of the book's purposes is to arrive at a grade on a report card, the book has another very important use. Select a quiet corner of an otherwise noisy music room or a bench in the park and read through the various evaluation criteria. You may find yourself saying, "This may be something I should work toward next semester," or "Maybe I should check to make sure I am fulfilling these criteria." The book then becomes a guide for further development and investigation rather than a rigid evaluation tool.

Part One of *Evaluation Programs for School Bands and Orchestras* discusses the various components of a school instrumental music program that can be evaluated by the 21 evaluation devices presented in Part Two, "The Criterion." Here is a brief description of what you'll find in Part One:

- Chapter 1 contains an explanation of the instrumental music program's curriculum and the literature that pertains to it. You'll also find a unique section on how to select the proper degree of difficulty of musical compositions for various performing groups and various types of performances they might present.

- Chapter 2 discusses the instrument, the rental programs, private lessons, class lessons, summer programs, the stage band, the marching band, scheduling, and the school music administrator's part in the overall picture.

- Chapter 3 covers public relations, public performances, and the preparation for performances. This includes such topics as rehearsal planning, rehearsal techniques, and selection of music that will introduce the students to various styles and periods of music.

- Chapter 4 gives details as to what makes for good school music facilities, equipment, and materials, as well as the kinds of supplies that can make the instrumental music teacher's job an efficiently run enterprise.
- Chapter 5 shows how you can present a complete picture of the instrumental music department's offerings and how it is making use of taxpayer funds.

Some of the questions that can be answered by using *Evaluation Programs for School Bands and Orchestras* are:

- How can I select the best possible method books for my students to be sure they will acquire all the technical skills they might need?
- What should I be looking for when I select music for my groups to perform?
- Is there a definitive method for deciding how difficult a certain piece of music is?
- What can I look for if I want something that will really challenge my students?
- When giving private lessons, what should be done to ensure the students are getting their money's worth?
- A lot of students grumble about marching band. What can I do to improve what we are doing so that some of the grumbling might stop?
- I am now a department chairperson. What should I expect of myself so that I can do the best possible job for those in my department?
- I want to make sure I am giving my students a wide range of music in their performances. How can I make a survey to check on my selections?
- I wonder how the audiences at my concerts really feel about what is being done. They applaud their youngsters, but do they really believe this is educational?
- Sometimes I wonder just how effective my last rehearsal was. How can I check this?
- What can I do to insure that I am making the most effective use of rehearsal time?

A special feature of this book is Part Three, which includes a curriculum outline and scales to help you accurately assess *each* student's performance in the band or orchestra.

In short, *Evalauation Programs for School Bands and Orchestras* gives you all the information you need to evaluate your instrumental music program. You will then make your programs more successful and your students vitally interested in, and excited about, music.

Russell A. Pizer

Contents

Part Two
THE CRITERIA • 49

Part Three
APPENDIXES • 197

INDEX • 217

Part 1

The School Instrumental Music Program

Chapter 1

The Curriculum

SEE: Page 67. Criterion Model #1: Criteria for Evaluating an Instrumental Music Program.

Though it is mandatory in most schools for the classroom teacher to have a curriculum and follow monthly, weekly, and even daily lesson plans, this is not always the case with the band and orchestra director. However, a carefully structured instrumental music program is just as important as a carefully structured math class, English class, or history class. To have a carefully structured program, some kind of plans are an absolute necessity. Too often, the director of a school band or orchestra goes blindly from one performance to another, guided only by what will be performed at the next public performance or competition-festival.

CURRICULUM OUTLINE

The first step toward a structured program is a curriculum outline. A curriculum outline can simply be a list of compositions the director would like to have the band or orchestra perform over the next three or four years. This would not be a static list, but one that can be altered or rearranged to suit the desires of the director, the needs of the students, or to make use of new publications.

A simple curriculum outline should include what lesson books a student should study for each year of training. This does not have to be a static list either, but merely a guide as to what the teacher would like to have students accomplish for each year of training.

A sophisticated curriculum can take many hours of thought and study, and may sit on a shelf unused. However, by drawing up a sophisticated curriculum a teacher can find out a lot about the subject being taught. It forces the teacher to seriously consider that which is being taught as opposed to what the students should be learning.

Following is a format for a very sophisticated curriculum outline.

    I. LEVEL OF LEARNING

    II. COURSE DESCRIPTION

    III. GENERAL OBJECTIVES

    IV. UNIT TOPICS
        1. (first unit topic)
        2. (second unit topic)
        3. (third unit topic)

    V. TIME ALLOCATIONS

    VI. UNIT TOPIC #1
        A. Importance
        B. Overview of the unit
        C. General objectives
        D. Performance objectives
        E. Behavioral objectives
        F. Motivating activities
        G. Culminating activities
        H. Evaluating activities

    VII. UNIT TOPIC #2
        as unit topic #1

    VIII. UNIT TOPIC #3
        as unit topic #1

    (etc.)

A complete version of this type of outline is provided in Appendix A. It is for a fifth grade beginning band instrumental class.

SELECTING MATERIALS

The steps in organizing a curriculum would deal with determining what instructional materials are to be used in the development of the instrumentalist. It would include everything from the instrumental books to be used with the beginning band and orchestra members to the music selected for concerts. The instructional materials would include (1) which books students should be able to successfully complete, and at which level; (2) what kinds of music they will be offered; and (3) how the quality of the music would be rated.

METHOD BOOK EVALUATION

SEE: Page 106. Criterion Model #2: Method Book Evaluation.

The proper selection of a beginning method book does not necessarily spell the success or failure of a beginning instrumental program. A good teacher can make successful use of almost any kind of instruction book. It is true, however, that the more suited a method is for a particular situation the more efficient the teacher can be.

There are basically three types of approaches used by authors of beginning band methods. [This would also include approaches used by orchestra methods.]

1. Whole Note Approach—The first dozen or two lines (sometimes the first few pages) are whole notes with whole rests interspersed. The advocates of this system say that this approach allows for the beginning of a firm embouchure (or bowing position) through the use of sustained tones. Also, in this type of book, the children are not confused either with articulation (or bowing) or the motor responses necessary for moving from one note to another in quick succession.

2. Melody Approach—In this type of book, notes are presented with an introductory explanation. The first actual lines of music to be played by the student contain all of these introductory notes in some sort of a melody.

3. Rote-to-Note—This method includes such ideas as the first several lessons being devoted to playing the instruments using letters or numbers without the use of a staff or rhythmic notation.

TYPES OF METHODS

The manner in which the students will be grouped for lessons also determines to a great extent the type of instructional book to be used: homogeneous (class lessons of like instruments), heterogeneous (band/orchestra method), or private (similar to a class lesson book for like instruments).

The differences in the methods center around the order in which notes are introduced. With the class method, the most natural progression of notes can be followed. However, in a band/orchestra method, many compromises must be made. In a band method, the clarinets and cornets are usually started on middle C, and proceed upward to second line G, (Bb concert to F concert), the flutes will have to start on third line Bb, move to C and on upward—going over the break to fourth line D.

It will be helpful to make up a chart in order to compare books. Before any evaluation can be made, one has to decide just what purpose the method book should serve—merely a vehicle for instrumental instruction, or a nearly complete text.

Some methods contain almost no explanation, except for a fingering chart. At the other extreme, there is one method that contains (in the teacher's manual and conductor's score) fifty-two pages on methods of teaching each instrument."*

SELECTING MUSIC FOR EDUCATION

In some respects, a music teacher's position in the overall scheme of education is not too unlike that of a teacher of world literature.

A student entering a junior high or high school class in literature, or an elementary student whose teacher starts a unit in reading, should not expect to read and study the contents of comic books, even though comic books are more popular with children than hard-cover books. Comic books far out-sell books by Tolstoy or Hemingway etc., in volumes purchased by young people.

Students in a properly structured literature class are not given what they want to read or what is the most popular fare of the day. They are given that which is worthy of study because it has lasting value—that which is considered "classic" or has the quality of becoming a "classic." The conscientious teacher of world literature does not keep an eye on the "Top 20" or "Top 40" from a commercially oriented chart of popularity that changes regularly to encourage sales.

The position many music teachers take is that they must "relate to the students on their own level." Too often, this means letting the students have their "own music." Perhaps it is a good idea to begin at their level, i.e., with "peer-popular" music. An approach along this line may be good if it ultimately leads to the classics. However, this "relating" must be done specifically in an effort to take students from where they are to where they should be. This is supposed to be the essence of education!

SELECTION PROCESS

The process for selecting performance materials has to have a multi-faceted approach. These can be divided into two main categories: (1) the performers' musical maturity and (2) the listeners' receptivity levels.

The category of musical maturity of the performance includes: (a) the group's overall technical skills and (b) their musical knowledge that can be applied to a performance via their technical skills.

The musical maturity intrinsic in a musical composition is most often represented by its Degree of Difficulty (*DoD*). The full implications and meaning of the acronym *DoD* will be discussed at length below.

*© 1971 by The Instrumentalist Co. Reprinted by permission from *The Instrumentalist*, August, 1971. Subscriptions are available from The Instrumentalist Co., 200 Northfield Road, Northfield, Illinois, USA.

Note: There are several ways of referring to the various levels of difficulty of a musical composition. Most methods provide for six levels or degrees of difficulty. Below is a chart that correlates all the various systems. This book uses the acronym: *DoD*.

DoD-1 = VE	= Very easy	= Grade I	= Class D
DoD-2 = E	= Easy	= Grade II	= Class C
DoD-3 = M	= Medium	= Grade III	= Class B
DoD-4 = MD	= Moderately difficult	= Grade IV	= Class A
DoD-5 = D	= Difficult	= Grade V	= Class AA
DoD-6 = VD	= Very difficult	= Grade VI	= Class AAA

In most cases (but not all), the degree of difficulty (shown by the *DoD* number) also represents the composition's musical maturity level.

The exception would be the following. Some early Classical works may appear technically easy, but they are musically difficult. This is especially true because too many people (even many schooled musicians) do not completely understand different musical styles.

Also tied to the *DoD* number is a composition's fatigue factor, discussed below. The higher the *DoD* number, the more physical stamina it takes to perform the work "in public." Not being knowledgeable about or aware of fatigue factors in musical compositions can result in a very poor education experience.

STAMINA FACTOR

The "Stamina Factor" could also be called the "fatigue factor" or the "maturity factor."

Like long-distance runners, instrumentalists need to develop varying degrees of stamina to perform compositions in different *DoD* categories.

A musical composition that is labeled *DoD*-6 would be like the Boston Marathon for the band/orchestra members. To finish a *DoD*-6 the musicians must build up very high levels of stamina over long hours, days, and years of practice.

A runner who wants to compete in the Boston Marathan must build up very high levels of stamina over long hours, days, weeks, and years of workouts. This does not come easily and cannot be hurried. It has to be a slow, methodical development. It cannot be forced on the body. The body, like a band member's embouchure or a string player's bow arm, takes careful nurturing over long periods of time to be able to meet the requirements of a "long" musical composition.

Up to this point, nothing has been said about the degree of success of the marathoner or the musician in their respective endeavors.

A marathon runner who is truly serious about competing successfully, i.e., finishing with a good time, has to "study" marathon running very carefully and in great detail. He/she cannot just put on running shoes one day and decide: "Next month I think I'll run in the Boston Marathon." That "study" of marathon running has to be methodically and meticulously applied over many months and years in order to build up the musculature and respiratory stamina necessary to complete the marathon. A runner who does not condition his/her body properly may be able to go only a few miles before collapsing.

Likewise, the student musician who does not have the physical and musical maturity (it might be called) to complete a *DoD-6* will experience severe frustration, if not abject failure.

The problem of stamina, fatigue, or maturity is more obvious with a soloist than with a full band or orchestra performance. In example:

A ninth grader—we will call him Edward—appears before an adjudicator with his brand new professional quality trombone, his accompanist, and his *DoD-5* solo.

Two years ago he played a *DoD-3* and did an A-number-1 job. Last year he played a *DoD-4* and did a "pretty darn good" job for an eighth grader. He didn't want to play another *DoD-4* solo this year, so he moved up to *DoD-5*.

Ed is a bright boy. He regularly goes to symphony orchestra concerts in The City with his parents. He has a modest collection of classical recordings and even a few recordings of trombone solos. In fact, the solo he is performing before the adjudicator is one that is on one of his albums. He has even had a few lessons on this solo with the first trombonist in The City Symphony Orchestra.

Ed practices about thirty to forty minutes almost every day. When he does not have too much homework, he will practice an hour or more. On weekends, he will practice two or three hours altogether. He sandwiches his practice sessions between his household chores, his favorite TV programs, and visits to his brother and sister-in-law and their children. He is also involved in the church youth fellowship.

As Ed begins his solo performance, things go extremely well. His intonation is exceptionally good. His tone is full and quite sonorous for a ninth grader on his new trombone. Some of the more difficult passages on page two go quite well—especially for a ninth grader. However, toward the bottom of page two, he really messes up a long series of sixteenth notes. He seems to be a little flustered. However, there are sixteen measures of rest coming up. That should give him some time to regain some of the composure he had earlier.

During the rests, Ed rubs his lips with the back of his hand several times, lets the water out of his slide—several times—and fidgets with the slide. There is a very pronounced ring around his lips from the pressure of the mouthpiece. Ed "putters" his lips several times and pulls on them as if trying to restore circulation.

He will soon be at the recapitulation, so he should have smooth sailing.

However, he misses his entrance after the rests. His accompanist has to replay the lead-in measures a second time.

In his hurry to get the trombone up to his mouth, Ed almost knocks over his music stand.

After this bungled start, his composure seems to have all but vanished. Things now begin going from bad to worse. The sides of Ed's embouchure collapse. Air begins escaping around the sides of his lips. His tone disintegrates, as does his intonation.

Should the adjudicator stop Ed's agony? No need. He will self-destruct in a few more minutes. Air is now escaping through his nose. This scenario is an example (that is far too common) of ambition that exceeds the stamina factor.

When a band or orchestra performs overly ambitious *DoD*'s, an astute adjudicator can detect when the disintegrating effects of fatigue begin setting in.

Such failed efforts are, obviously, educationally disastrous. They are not only physically taxing, but can be psychologically damaging to students' egos. This in turn adversely affects the students' attitudes toward the whole field of instrumental music.

Potentially superior musicians, who experience such ego shattering performances too often or in a high impact situation, may unconsciously decide to "throw in the towel" at the next possible opportunity.

Obviously, the way to prevent this from occurring is to set aside the *DoD*-generated ego. It must be substituted by sound educational considerations. These considerations must be solely based on the student's musical maturity.

CHECKING STAMINA LEVELS

Here is a very simple way to check to see if an individual or group has the sufficient stamina to perform a composition "in public." (Some of the items may seem redundant, but they are repeated so there will be no mistake as to the intent of this process.)

Play the composition (to be used "in public"). . . .

- in its entirety,
- without any stops whatsoever (except for notated rests),
- from "top to bottom"
- three times in immediate succession

so that each successive play-through is not separated by more than three minutes of rest. The time between play-through must be only enough to get a "quick" breath, perhaps let the saliva out of the trumpets, trombones, and bassoons, and swab out the clarinets.

If this procedure cannot be completed or is not done, the performance will probably be a disaster in some way or another.

When a group or soloist tries to prepare a composition for performance that is well above the appropriate stamina level, it takes so much time to learn the composition there is just no time to play the composition all the way through several times. So often, the composition is played in bits and pieces hundreds of times, but never in its entirety until it is put up for the "acid test." Sometimes the first complete play-through is at a "dress rehearsal." Even a play-through at a dress rehearsal is not a true test of a group's stamina because there are not a lot of stress factors that will arise in performance. The stress factor of a performance adds greatly to the overall fatigue that will exert itself on everyone.

A young musician playing a solo for an adjudicator will have a tremendous number of added stress factors. This will be especially true if the soloist has never played his composition in front of anyone except his teacher and accompanist. Thus it is of the utmost importance that schools who have students participating in solo competition-festivals provide recitals before the events are to be held to provide a "dress rehearsal."

JUDGING QUALITY OF MUSIC

SEE: Page 112. Criterion Model #3: Check List for Judging Quality Music.

Whereas there may be some argument as to what is considered a "good piece of music" and what is not, there are certain aspects of musical compositions—like those which would be performed by a band or orchestra—that can be judged. Criterion Model #3 provides a "Check List for Judging Quality Music" that contains eighteen key items. Not all compositions can meet all the criteria, but should meet a considerable number of them.

To what extent this criteria is used for each selection is not determinable herein. Perhaps its value comes in just knowing, or being able to read through a list of things that can be important when looking for quality in a musical composition.

Note: The reader is referred to an extensive discussion of this question in the book titled: *Building A Superior School Band Library* by Lawrence J. Intravia (published by Parker Publishing Co.). This books has a chapter titled: "Eight Criteria in Selecting Outstanding Concert Literature." (Although this book is out of print, you may be able to find a copy in your town or school library.)

THE DoD

SEE: Page 114. Criterion Model #4: Defining the *DoD* of Band Compositions.

Many music publishers provide a degree of technical and musical difficulty of a musical composition (*DoD*) on the scores to their musical compositions. (See page 205 for the different classification systems.) There are several state music association manuals and lists by which this information can be garnered also. However, sometimes the lists from different sources show different *DoD*'s. There are even examples where the *DoD* in a state manual is changed from one year to the next. This occurs because many, if not all, agencies or individuals that set the *DoD* use totally subjective criteria.

Criterion Model #4 (Defining the *DoD* of Band Compositions) is an objective method for arriving at the degree of difficulty of band compositions. This method is very complicated and involves processes that would consume a considerable amount of time to evaluate a single composition. However, it does provide a completely accurate and verifiable standard.

The items in Model #4 would have to be adapted to the different types of ensembles: full orchestra, string quartets, woodwind quintets, et al. Also, such criteria would need to be adapted to arrive at an objective method for establishing the degree of difficulty of solo materials.

THE DoD FOR PERFORMANCE

There are three broad areas of consideration when selecting materials for groups or individuals to perform.

1. The *DoD* as it relates to a group or individual Level of Performance Proficiency (*LoPP*).
2. The purpose to which the composition is to be put.
3. The quality of that music.

The information that follows will be directed toward a large performing group like a school orchestra, but also applies to the school band and small ensembles like a string quartet, woodwind quintet, or brass octet. It also applies to an individual—particularly in the selection of solo materials for recitals and competitions.

Before beginning the selection process, it is necessary to have an understanding of the group's "mean" *LoPP*.

The use of the word "mean" in connection with *LoPP* (written "mean-*LoPP*") refers to a point halfway between two extremes of performance proficiency. The mean-*LoPP* is a subjectively perceived performance level halfway between a refined performance and a muddled, rhythmically and stylistically inaccurate reading that lacks an acceptable semblance of fluency.

It is not necessary to establish a definitive mean-*LoPP*, but to have at least a mentally perceived understanding of such is very important. Past performance history will give a fairly accurate picture of a group's *LoPP*, if care is exercised when looking at the date. Historical data however, can give a distorted picture of a group's or soloist's "true" *LoPP*. The "true" *LoPP* in most cases is one *DoD* higher (more difficult) than the mean-*LoPP*.

Conceivably, a band or orchestra could have a record of receiving *LoPP*-A in *DoD*-6* for several years in a row at the state competition-festival and yet not approach that level in terms of real performance proficiency.

This situation can occur because some band and orchestra directors are obsessed with performing *DoD*-6 music. In order to do this, these directors are willing to spend all year working on compositions to be performed at the annual competition-festival. Students in such bands and orchestras become little more than humanoid versions of trained seals.

The mean-*LoPP* is that *DoD* which can be sight-read under the following conditions:

The composition that is sight-read must be performed:

1. with some degree of fluency
2. with considerable rhythmic accuracy
3. without any stop to get the group together again; the group must play from the beginning to the end of the composition without having problems staying together
4. without verbal directions from the conductor during the read-through†

If the conductor finds it necessary to call out rehearsal letters or numbers, hold up fingers indicating the rehearsal number coming up, pounding on the music stand to enforce the beat, etc., the students' effort cannot be counted as a legitimate play-through under these guidelines.

For example, if the school orchestra can successfully sight-read through a *DoD*-4 using the above criteria, the *DoD*-4 would be the group's mean-*LoPP*.

If the school's woodwind quintet tries to read through a *DoD*-5 but has to stop several times, this is well above their mean-*LoPP*. They should try a *DoD*-4 or *DoD*-3 to discover their proper mean-*LoPP*.

It is acknowledged that some groups or individuals may appear to have a greater propensity for sight reading. This may be the result of a higher level of overall skill. Perhaps it is because the teachers in these cases have given specific instruction in the skill of sight reading. (Sight reading *can* be taught.) Regardless of the reasons, such a group or individual would nevertheless have a proportionally higher true *LoPP*.

Under normal circumstances, it is educationally unsound to select any musical composition for performance that is two *DoD*'s higher than the mean-*LoPP*. Selecting a composition even one *DoD* higher than the mean-*LoPP* would give the students a considerable challenge—if that is the specific purpose behind the selection.

---

*NOTE: For purposes of the discussion, a *6A+* would be a "perfect" score given by an adjudicator at a music competition-festival in a composition that is "very difficult."
†Item #4 does not preclude a "talk through" of the composition before the play-through begins.

If an orchestra has a mean-*LoPP* of *DoD*-4, any attempt to perform a *DoD*-6 will only result in a lot of frustrated students. Rehearsals in such a case would be reduced to nothing more than rote training sessions. Incidentally, there is a considerable difference between rote training and rehearsing.

There is also the important factor of a group's musical maturity (other than pure technical prowess) that should be considered. If the group's mean-*LoPP* is *DoD*-4, it is not likely their musical maturity and stamina would be equal to a composition rated as *DoD*-6.

The orchestra director who has a group with a mean-*LoPP* of *DoD*-4 that tries to prepare a *DoD*-6 for performance is like the English teacher having eighth graders read Shakespeare's *King Lear* in the original version. While they will be able to recognize most of the individual words set down by Shakespeare, it is unlikely that the students would be able to comprehend *King Lear*.

The second set of variables is the purpose for which a composition is to be used. The purposes could be one or more of the following:

1. for historical understanding
2. for stylistic understanding
3. for improved technical skills
4. for improved sight reading skills
5. for competition-festival participation
6. for a "classical" concert
7. for a "pops" concert
8. for a demonstration or recruiting concert
9. for a utilitarian program like a school assembly

There is absolutely no education rationale that would require a school orchestra or band director to select any one *DoD* for all the above categories. Here are some varying rationale for selecting various *DoD*—depending on the purposes to which a composition is to be put.

Of the nine purposes given above, numbers 5 and 6 are probably the only ones that would use a *DoD* higher than the mean-*LoPP*. Purposes number 1 and 2 should be one *DoD* lower than the mean-*LoPP*. Purpose number 2 should definitely be one *DoD* lower, if not two. Such a training vehicle should be well within the group's technical abilities and musical maturity.

Purpose number 4 should start one, two, or even three *DoD*'s lower than the mean-*LoPP* depending on the perceived level of abilities. The lower the initial *DoD*, the higher the immediate profile of success when first starting to do training in sight reading.

Purposes number 7 and 8 should consider not just the group's musical maturity but that of the potential audience. For example, if the school orchestra is being taken to the elementary schools to play for school assemblies, it would be a grave mistake to play even one movement of a Brahms symphony, even if the group is fully capable of playing such at a high *LoPP*. (There are, of course, always exceptions to a generalization like this.)

Chapter 2

The Program and Its Schedule

SEE: Page 71 and 89. Criterion Model #1: Criteria for Evaluating an Instrumental Music Program.

It has often been said that a good teacher can achieve results even under adverse conditions. While this may be true, a good teacher can be even more effective under ideal conditions. The teacher's enthusiasm and inventiveness can compensate for many inadequacies in materials, supplies, even in equipment and facilities. In this case the adage, "Necessity is the mother of invention," can make up for the many things that might not be immediately available either in quality or quantity.

There are probably few (if any) teachers who would admit they have an ideal teaching situation. Another adage is apropos here: "The grass is always greener on the other side of the fence." There is almost always something that is needed or desired to assist with the teaching process. Though having a well-lighted, fully-equipped, air-conditioned, spacious rehearsal area with individual practice rooms is highly desirable, it is not what makes for a concert performance of superior quality. There are school districts that have ideal facilities and lots of equipment that do not turn out proficient, musically knowledgeable players.

Some of the items contained in Criterion Model #1, "Criteria for Evaluating an Instrumental Musical Program," may be seen as being too idealistic or overly ambitious. They may be seen as reaching for that "pie in the sky." While this may be true, it is also true that the nature and psyche of the creature known as *Homo sapient* is one who dreams—one who is constantly looking over the next horizon. It is therefore the intent of this criteria to look over that horizon.

Criteria Model #1 is not meant to point an accusatory finger at anyone, but rather to give direction even to the instrumental program that for all practical purposes is considered highly successful. If nothing more, those pages could assist the director of a highly successful program to show that indeed he has been highly successful. That is, after all, the basis of what is called "accountability."

INSTRUMENTAL RENTAL PROGRAMS

> See: Pages 73–74. Item #IIID & IIIE of The Criterion Model #1: Criteria for Evaluating an Instrumental Music Program.

With the widespread concept of equal opportunity for all, it has become a necessity for a school system to have a variety of instrumental rental programs so each and every child, whatever his family income, can participate in the instrumental program. In an effort to allow all children to participate, many schools—in addition to a rental-purchase plan—also have a limited number of school-owned instruments. However, in many instances it turns out that the only instruments the school owns are the larger ones that would not otherwise be purchased by parents. This situation does help solve the problem of instrumentation but it solves it in an unfair manner. It means that the children from fairly affluent families play flutes, clarinets, alto saxophones, trumpets, and violins while those from poorer ones play the lower clarinets and saxophones, euphoniums, tubas and lower strings. It will also be observed that the poorer children end up playing instruments of poor quality—at least in most schools—while the more affluent students in the same beginning classes have nice new and shiny instruments.

Another situation arises when a child owns his own instrument but is transferred to another either by his choice or because his ability on his own instrument is not an asset to the group. Oftentimes a rather poor clarinetist can be turned into an average or even above average bassoonist, bass clarinetist, saxophonist, or even oboist. This may also be the case with a poor trumpet player if he is placed on a larger mouthpiece brass instrument.*

The criteria include information for three different kinds of rental programs: that which would include school-owned instruments, those from a commercial company, and a combination of the two.

---

*© 1968 by The Instrumentalist Co. Reprinted by permission from *The Instrumentalist*, November, 1968. Subscriptions are available from The Instrumentalist Co., 200 Northfield Road, Northfield, Illinois, USA.

TECHNIC INSTRUCTION

SEE: Page 75. Items #IIIF, G, & H of Criterion Model #1: Criteria for Evaluating an Instrumental Music Program.

The most important student-oriented aspect of an instrumental music program is the giving of technic instruction in private or class lessons.

Too often, this aspect of the program is totally ignored after the students get out of the beginners' classes or graduate from elementary school. As soon as a violinist or cellist can play a few notes beyond the beginning lesson, he or she is given the school orchestra music that is to be used in the next concert. Even college music education courses do not seem to place much emphasis on this aspect. In too many cases, the only training given is via the requirement that music majors study a major instrument with a private instructor and minor instruments in class lessons.

Formalized technic lessons often stop as soon as a child is capable of playing in the school band or orchestra. However, practicing band music and more band music does not a good musician make! If students are not given regular, specialized technic lessons each and every year of their participation in the band or orchestra, they are being cheated by the teacher's short-term goals. This also means that if technic lessons are given (aside from band and orchestra practice), those lessons must not be devoted to practicing the band and orchestra music.

STUDENT EVALUATION

Two evaluation vehicles in The Criterion "Evaluating Private Lessons" (Model #5), and "Evaluating Class Lessons" (Model #6) are for students to fill out.

There has been much discussion and investigation into the value of having students evaluate their teachers. All the ramifications of such actions would fill several volumes and so will not be dealt with herein. There is a great deal of validity in such a practice, even though it might make a teacher a bit nervous. For this reason, these two vehicles (and the others in this book) need not be used universally with all the students or classes as a regular course of evaluation. However, as a personal checklist they can give the teacher seeking to do the best possible job a source of candid information.

PRIVATE LESSONS

SEE: Page 75. Items #IIIF, G, & H of Criterion Model #1: Criteria for Evaluating an Instrumental Music Program.

If any teacher ever ponders the question, what one thing would do the most to provide for a fine sounding band or orchestra?, the answer would be private lessons. There is a direct correlation between the quality of musical performances of bands and orchestras and the number of students in those groups who are taking private lessons. There is no substitute, when considering the performance proficiency of a band or orchestra, for having such a group full of fine individual performers. And, an individual cannot become a fine performer if he does not develop his skills under the tutelage of a trained specialist in the particular instrument or instrumental family. There is no substitute for the oboe player in the orchestra being able to study with a specialist on the oboe. A cellist cannot learn all the finer points of bow technic by simply rehearsing with the orchestra day after day and practicing his or her parts at home.

It would be too great a burden financially on the schools to employ sufficient numbers of specialists to give all the band and orchestra members private lessons. However, realizing the importance of private lessons, many schools provide a service of helping students to find specialists. If the school is in or near a metropolitan center that has a professional or semi-professional orchestra, a rich source of teachers is usually available. A rural school may even find it advisable to import some specialists for a few hours a week for after-school lessons at the parents' expense or provide the school's facilities for Saturday lessons.

CLASS LESSONS

> SEE: Page 75. Items #IIIF, G, & H of Criterion Model #1: Criteria for Evaluating an Instrumental Music Program.
>
> AND: Page 143. Criterion Model #6: Evaluating Class Lessons.

Because schools generally cannot afford to give private lessons on school time, class lessons can and must be part of the overall instrumental program. Class lessons in groups of four to six like instruments are justifiable and extremely valuable to the students in the instrumental music program. To evaluate such, Criterion Model #7 (Evaluating Private Lessons) has been altered slightly to account for this kind of group activity.

SUMMER PROGRAM

> See: Page 83. Item #IV of Criterion Model #1: Criteria for Evaluating an Instrumental Music Program.

A summer instrumental music program can be a boon or bane. The boon is that a summer program can be a time for highly productive and concentrated study that is not possible during the regular school year, when students must make choices of whether to practice music or study their science lessons. It also affords the time to provide course offerings that are not possible during the regular school year. These would include such things as music theory, harmony, in-depth care of an instrument, etc.

A summer program is by far the best time to start beginners. Such a program would allow for whatever time is necessary for instruction. If the teacher so desired, and there is ample evidence that this can be tremendously advantageous, the beginning classes could meet every day. Conceivably, the students would leave their instruments in school for the first few weeks. This approach essentially means the beginning would be practicing only under the watchful eye of the teacher. As such, bad habits are less likely to become prevalent.

However, summer programs can be the cause of further conflict over finances between the Board of Education, the school administration, the music teacher(s), and the parents. A budget that is already too small may be more taxed by the addition of paying out monies for such a program. Conceivably, parents of students could object to a non-funded or partially funded program on the grounds that they are already paying enough for their children's education through the school taxes.

The offering of a summer program also puts students on a schedule that does not allow a reprieve from the constant pressure to practice. While it is acknowledged that a summer layoff from the study and practice of a musical instrument is not in keeping with the concepts of a dedicated musician, a summer program may prove a negative factor on some of the less dedicated members of the band and orchestra. They may rather quit the program altogether than have to face a year-round practice and rehearsal schedule.

SCHEDULE

Summer instrumental music programs can be structurally classed as being: (1) minimal, (2) partial, (3) complete, and (4) maximum. Financially, they will fall into six categories: (1) non-funded, (2) tacitly partially funded, (3) peer group partially funded, (4) peer group totally funded, (5) partially school funded, and (6) fully funded.

A program that would be considered minimal/non-funded would be the type whereby the instrumental music teacher gives only private lessons during the summer. These lessons would be given in a facility other than at the school, such as the teacher's or students' homes.

A summer program of private lessons that is paid for by the student, whereby the teacher uses the school, would be in the category of the minimal program with tacitly partial funding depending upon whether the Board of

Education gives specific approval for the program or merely allows it to occur. It would be in the "partial funding" category because any use of school facilities requires some concern of school personnel, monies, or materials. The teacher will cost the schools some funds just by being in the building, if only for the use of the school's rest rooms that will need to be supplied by the custodial staff. It is also classed here because some of the students would be using school-owned instruments. In addition, lessons might include some materials from the school's instrumental music library as well as electricity for lights.

A *partial program* would be the type whereby only lessons and some type of concert band or orchestra rehearsals are held.

A *complete program* would be defined as that type which is normally the offering given during the regular school year.

A *peer group funded program* would be the type by which funds are raised either by the students involved or by donations solicited from the community.

A *maximum program* would be the type that is not only instrumentally oriented by way of lessons and band or orchestra rehearsals, but also offers such things as music theory, history, acoustics, etc. This would entail not only beginning instrumental classes, but an exploratory class as well. It would essentially be a complete conservatory-of-music program.

Conceivably, two or more school districts could join together for a summer program. For example, two or three high school marching bands could jointly rent a boy scout camp after their season is closed to have a pre-school band camp. If the orchestra director in Town *A* is an accomplished violinist and the orchestra director in Town *B*, six miles away, is an accomplished cellist, they could hold joint programs thereby making best use of both teachers' special talents.

STAGE BAND

> See: Page 86. Item #V of Criterion Model #1: Criteria for Evaluating an Instrumental Music Program.

As originally conceived, the stage band was the type of organization known in the late 1930s and early 1940s as a dance band of the kind used by Glenn Miller, Tommy Dorsey, Guy Lombardo, etc. Upon its entrance into the educational system in the late 1960s, the designation "dance band" was dropped in part because it would have faced opposition by certain church groups. Others did not want the "corrupting" influences of the dance hall coming into the schools. Some band directors just wanted to give this type of ensemble a more sophisticated sounding title. It thus took on such designations as: stage band, jazz band, jazz ensemble, jazz repertory ensemble, etc., and, to get additional appeal from some elements of the student population in the mid 1970s—jazz-rock ensemble.

Originally, the instrumentation of this kind of group consisted of:

2 alto saxophones	4 trumpets
2 tenor saxophones	4 trombones
1 baritone saxophone	1 string bass
1 piano	1 dance drum set
1 acoustical guitar	

With the rise in popularity of rock music, these groups added hundred of decibels of sound through electronic amplification. The string bass became electrically amplified or replaced by an electric bass with its separate amplifier and speaker system. Further, the acoustical guitar was replaced by at least one electric guitar and the piano was substituted with an electronic keyboard of some kind.

PROS AND CONS OF STAGE BANDS

Those who advocate such a program, claim the music is such that it stimulates interest in the entire music program. This is true, so the advocates claim, by having the stage band perform for a wider variety of audiences than is possible with the full band or orchestra.

The advocates of the stage band also claim that such a group gives the students training (as do other "small ensembles") in developing individual responsibility—responsibility for performing a part that is not duplicated by many others in a section.

These same advocates will say the stage band increases the members' abilities to listen carefully and blend their instrumental tonal qualities with the others in the group. There is also the argument that only in a stage band can the instrumental students learn to improvise.

Those who are not advocates of stage band programs feel that all too often, schools that have such a program usually end up placing greater emphasis on that "elite" group. As a result, the stage band program tends to get out of hand at the expense of the other performing groups.

If music teachers believe the stage band is of value because it provides "small ensemble" training, and all it entails, why don't they usually provide other "small ensembles" for their students? The instrumental music teacher who has a stage band as part of his/her "small ensemble" offering should have a complete program—not just a stage band. This should consist of at least two string quartets, two clarinet quartets, a woodwind quintet, two brass quartets, and a percussion ensemble—or some such combination. However, truly active small ensemble program, which would benefit a greater percentage of the students than just having an "elite group" would be very time consuming. No one could criticize such a program, as many do, when a stage band is the only "small ensemble" offered.

Junior High School Stage Bands

There are those who have transported the stage band program from being a group for advanced senior high school players to the junior high school. Far too often a junior high school stage band is a ludicrous endeavor. Whereas there is some music composed specifically with young students in mind, this fare is far from adequate in number and quality. As a result, the director of a junior high school group feels duty bound to play some "well known" tunes that require mature performance abilities.

The director who institutes such a program at the junior high level must not truly understand young embouchure or does so to satisfy his or her own ego. It often appears that such a junior high stage band director may not be much more than a frustrated professional musician who is trying to psychologically compensate him- or herself at the expense of the students. This is done by arranging to be at the helm of that which he or she probably cannot hope to achieve outside of the school.

Therefore, rather than a stage band, the junior high school instrumental music program should first have active clarinet quartets, brass quartets, et al. After these are in place and thriving, then perhaps a junior high stage band would be apropos.

REHEARSAL GUIDELINES

SEE: Page 145. Criterion Model #7: Evaluating Stage Band Rehearsals.

The check list used for "Evaluating Stage Band Rehearsals" was drawn by George Wiskirchen. He suggests that the director "seek the answers to these questions honestly." (George Wiskirchen, "Rehearsing a School Jazz Band," *Jazz in the 70's—A High School Teacher's Guide.* Elkhart, IN: The Selmer Co., 22.)

MARCHING BAND EVALUATION

SEE: Page 151. Criterion Model #8: Student Evaluation of the Marching Band.

There are many problems that relate to the marching band that could be checked out by asking the band members specifically how they feel about various items. The seventeen items on the "Student Evaluation of the Marching Band" (Criterion Model #8) would be helpful to a director by giving guidance for further ment of individual activities as well as for the management of those who aid him or her in various capacities.

In addition to the seventeen questions, an open-ended response is called for via "How can the participation in the marching band be made more beneficial, rewarding, and/or enjoyable?"

Scheduling

> SEE: Page 89. Criterion Model #1: Criteria for evaluating an Instrumental Music Program.

Scheduling of the instrumental groups can be a tremendous problem. It all comes down to whether those doing the scheduling truly understand the process and whether they are sympathetic to, and understand the needs of, the band and orchestra. Scheduling in the high school is a particular problem because there is not another course that requires such a large number of students who come from every grade level and must meet as a single unit. Added to this, problems are compounded if the school has an orchestra in which the band members participate to fill out the wind and percussion parts.

Proper scheduling for the groups thus depends to the greatest extent on whether the school's administration looks favorably on this program and will put some priorities on the program's needs. Sometimes it may be necessary for the band/orchestra director to become immediately involved in the scheduling process in order to get the time slots needed.

On the elementary level, problems abound because too often the classroom teacher has students coming and going all day long. He or she rarely gets to have all of the pupils in his or her class at any one moment. Having students go in and out of the classroom with their musical instruments in hand is a reminder that a big cause of frustration is the band and orchestra—not a nice attitude to be engendering—even though it cannot be helped.

MUSIC DEPARTMENT ADMINISTRATOR

> SEE: Page 64. Criterion Model #1: Criteria for Evaluating an Instrumental Music Program.
>
> AND: Page 171. Criterion Model #13: Music Department Administrator Evaluation.

Whereas the "Criteria for Evaluating an Instrumental Program" (Criterion Model #1) is somewhat of a public document regarding the responsibilities of the music department administration, the "Music Department Administrator Evaluation" (Criterion Model #13) is not.

The "Music Department Administrator Evaluation" is somewhat akin to the students evaluating the teacher. This vehicle is designed for the teachers to evaluate their supervisor. The information gleaned from this vehicle would be for the sole use of the administrator, as the results would be very personal and could even be ego-shattering.

Chapter 3

Public Relations,
Public Performance,
and the Preparation

PUBLIC RELATIONS

SEE: Page 154. Criterion Model #9: Evaluating Public Relations Strategies.

Developing Public Relations (PR) strategies is an important part of a band or orchestra director's job. Such strategies would include both internal and external concerns. (PR is a general term used to describe any efforts to gain attention, interest, or support from school officials, the community, and parents, as well as student participants.)

Unlike other subjects in the school (except the "sports department"), band and orchestra directors have to do a great deal of PR work.

Depending on the situation, internal PR strategies might start with periodic programs for Kindergarten classes. At the upper end of the music education PR spectrum, band and orchestra directors should be securing newspaper space and/ or radio and TV time for concerts, festivals, and competitions.

There is some information covering the area of PR in Criterion Model #1, Item I-D. However, that criterion is attributed as being the responsibility of the department chairperson. If there is no such titled person in the school system, most of those responsibilities would become foisted on the individual band and orchestra directors.

"Evaluating Public Relations Strategies" (Criterion Model #9) is for checking the PR ratings for an individual band or orchestra. As with other evaluation tools, the criteria could be used as a simple check list via asking the question: "Do I do this?", or "Don't I?", or "Should I be doing this?"

PARENT ASSOCIATIONS

SEE: Page 158. Criterion Model #10: Evaluating a Parent Association.

AND: Page 160. Criterion Model #11: Parent Priorities.

AND: Page 164. Criterion Model #12: Parent Evaluation of the Instrumental Music Program.

An officially organized parent association would be considered an external public relations vehicle. Such an organization can add greatly to the overall program if it is managed properly. If managed poorly, it can lead to all kinds of problems.

A loosely organized parent association can be used (and often is) to bypass normal school administrative channels. It has been seen that through careful selection of a parent association executive board, a band director can even manipulate an entire board of education (for several years). Such manipulations, however, ultimately prove disastrous for all concerned—especially the students.

The foundation upon which a well-run (and relatively trouble-free) parent association rests is a clearly defined set of operational guidelines in the form of association bylaws. It is also extremely important that the association knows that all activities must ultimately come under the scrutiny of the school's administration (and its lawyer)—the people who hire and fire the band/orchestra director.

"Evaluating a Parent Association" (Criterion Model #10) can be used as a kind of checklist for establishing or reviewing a parent association's modus operandi.

Two other vehicles, "Parent Priorities" (Criterion Model #11) and "Parent Evaluation of The Instrumental Music Program" (Model #12), can be used with or by a parent association.

"Parent Priorities" (Criterion Model #11) might be given out every two or three years at the last meeting of the school year. If the association's executive board so chooses, it could be used for a discussion at a general meeting.

The "Parent Evaluation of the Instrumental Music Program" would have to be used very judiciously. Perhaps it could be given just to the executive board members or a sample of the parents. The results may or may not necessarily be for general distribution and/or discussion. Also, this vehicle would probably not be used every year—maybe every two or three years.

SCHOOL CONCERTS

SEE: Page 88. Section VI of Criterion Model #1: Criteria for Evaluating an Instrumental Music Program.

The mark of an outwardly successful instrumental music program would be one whereby three or four concerts are given each year by each of the major performing groups. Each major performing group—the band and the orchestra—would each have its own nights. Additionally, there would be at least one yearly event that is set aside for recitals for soloists and small ensembles. This would most probably be just before those students are going to participate in the state's solo and ensemble competition-festival.

During band concerts there would be a few compositions performed by the school's woodwind quintet, perhaps the clarinet choir, the flute quartet, the brass octet, or the percussion ensemble that contains a keyboard instrument like a marimba or xylophone. If the concert is composed of half concert band and half jazz or rock band, this program's offerings might be in question.

During the orchestra concert there could be a string number. There might even be a few numbers performed by the school's string quartet and perhaps a solo by one of the outstanding players who is going to represent the school at the all-state.

A real test for the credibility of the school's performing groups would be to have them sight read a composition during a concert. This would be an especially good idea if the procedures were explained to the audience.

MUSICAL STYLES AND PERIODS

SEE: Page 175. Criterion Model #14: Musical Styles and Periods.

An instrumental music program's primary goal must be to give the students some knowledge about music. As such, it is important that the members of the performing groups be exposed to all kinds of styles in music as well as examples of literature from various historical periods. The form, "Survey on Styles and

Periods of Compositions Performed," (Criterion Model #14) gives a vehicle that can be used to survey this part of the program.

This vehicle contains a list of the various styles and periods and what kinds of compositions fit into which categories.

PUBLIC PERFORMANCE

> SEE: Page 181. Criterion Model #15: Concert Survey-Audience Reactions.

The test of a successful concert program might well be the number of persons in the audience who have no direct relationship to those performing; i.e., they come to the concert to hear the music, not simply to *see* their son, daughter, niece, nephew, grandchild, or whomever, perform. However, a good rule of thumb for figuring out how many people will be in an audience for a school concert is to multiply the number of students involved by the number three. This number provides for an audience of about three relatives for everyone involved.

Collecting periodic responses from the audience about the offerings being set forth can help in many ways. It will give a picture of whether there is a concert audience or a congregation of relatives. It gives the director some interesting insights into the makeup of that audience.

"Concert Survey–Audience Reactions" (Criterion Model #15) gives some questions that can be duplicated and placed in the concert program, handed out during intermission, and collected at the end of the concert. It could also be given out at the end of the concert and designated to be filled out while parents are waiting for the children to put their instruments away.

REHEARSAL

> SEE: Page 183. Criterion Model #16: Evaluation of Rehearsal Procedures.

When contemplating the process of analyzing procedures that are carried on by a conductor in the process of rehearsing, the following aspects have to be considered:

1. the rehearsal procedures
2. the methods and frequency of verbal directions
3. baton techniques
4. methodological approaches to rehearsing compositions
5. technical-musical aspects to be conveyed and considered

The rehearsal is a combination of eleven different procedural items. These items are somewhat interchangeable—some may be combined; some may be deleted from time to time or dropped altogether; some may receive more emphasis at different times of the year—all depending upon the program and upcoming events. The procedural items include:

1. pre-planning
2. rehearsal hall preparation
3. tune-up
4. warm-up
5. technical drills
6. familiar materials
7. rehearsal proper
8. sight reading
9. familiar pieces
10. training in musicianship
11. announcements

With the use of a rehearsal planning form like that shown in Figure 3–1, one can check to see the frequency with which many of these procedural items occur throughout the year. This inventory would have doubtful value except for a most general view of what might have been or is regularly deleted. This inventory would be done by listing those eleven items given above on a sheet of paper. Then, with the year's rehearsal planning forms in hand, make a check after each item when it occurs. Counting the number of checks after each item would point up whether the members of the band or orchestra were getting, for example, any training in sight reading. It would also show if the conductor only plays new pieces of a highly sophisticated nature and does not allow the members to play some music they might enjoy by virtue of their familiarity or "light classical" nature. Finally, it would show if the conductor is simply "hacking" away at new materials without giving the students any background knowledge about the compositions in general or providing any in-depth knowledge about music as an art form.

REHEARSAL PLANNING

> SEE: Page 183. Criterion Model #16: Evaluating of Rehearsal Procedures.

Much planning must go into a rehearsal if it is to flow smoothly. A band or orchestra director cannot simply walk into the rehearsal room when the bell sounds and begin conducting the music. "Evaluation of Rehearsal Procedures" (Criterion Model #16) gives an indication of some of the things that need to be

REHEARSAL PLANNING

WEEK OF:		M	TU	W	TH	F
Compo-sitions in Prepa-ration	1					
	2					
	3					
	4					
	5					
New Compos. &/or Sight Reading	6					
	7					
	8					
	9					
Technic						

Warm-ups, Tuning, Announcements, Musical Techniques and/or Procedures

Figure 3–1

considered. For purposes of evaluating the processes used by a director, the procedures would be the same as given in "Criteria for Evaluating an Instrumental Music Program" (Criterion Model #1).

CONDUCTORIAL DIRECTIVES

> SEE: Page 186. Criterion Model #17: Evaluating Conductorial Directives.

The items in the "Evaluating Conductorial Directives" (Criterion Model #17) are taken from Max Rudolf's book, *The Conductor's Art*, the items altered slightly to fit into a question-and-answer format. They center on the whys and wherefores of stopping a group for purposes of giving directions.*

CONDUCTORIAL TECHNIQUES

> SEE: Page 188. Criterion Model #18: Conducting Critique Sheet.

The next item that is concerned with conductorial techniques is best used with a video tape. There are just too many categories and items to be checked for even an independent observer. About the only way this tool could be used for a live performance is if at least two well-trained observers were to divide the criteria— one for the left hand and one for the right.

"Conducting Critique Sheet" (Criterion Model #18) does not allow for any convenient numerical outcomes. It would, however, give the individual some insights into the techniques being used, those that should be used, or those things that are being done that should not be done.

REHEARSAL PROCEDURE

> SEE: Page 190. Criterion Model #19: Rehearsal Procedures Monitoring.
>
> AND: Page 191. Criterion Model #20: Ensemble Techniques Monitoring.

Rehearsal Procedures Monitoring (Criterion Model #19) lists nine items that are the type of interactions that occur in the rehearsal. (A full discussion of each of

*Max Ruldolf, "Rehearsal Techniques," *The Conductor's Art*, edited by Carl Bamberger. New York: McGraw-Hill Book Co., 1965. Used with permission.

these items can be found in *How to Improve the High School Band Sound*, by Russell A. Pizer (West Nyack, N.Y.: Parker Pub. Co., 1976).

1. tutti playing
2. sectional playing
3. individual playing
4. divided sectional playing
5. isolated small group playing
6. repetitions of portions of a composition
7. verbal directions
8. non-verbal directions via conductoral techniques
9. questions by students for clarifications

Each of these items should be investigated as to their frequency of appearance or their lack of appearance during the course of a series of rehearsals.

"Rehearsal Procedures Monitoring" (Criterion Model #19) is a simple digital-outcome tool for checking these procedures. The monitoring can be done by the teacher himself through the use of a tape recording of the rehearsal. *Note*: If a colleague is not available, perhaps a senior who happens to be a section leader, the student conductor, or maybe even the organization's secretary could act as a "monitor." If a student teacher is available, this would make a convenient checker. It would also give the student teacher something to watch for during the course of a rehearsal.

The only problem with using a tape recording of the rehearsal is that number 8, non-verbal directions via conductorial techniques, would have to be deleted from the monitoring tool. With a video tape, however, it would be easily observable.

When using this vehicle, a check mark is to be made at least once a minute, or whenever a new item appears. If tutti playing lasts for five minutes, make a check mark each minute. If there is tutti playing and thirty seconds later an individual is asked to play three measures, a check mark is to be placed in the #3 category. If after only thirty-five seconds of that individual performance, tutti playing is resumed, another check mark is to be placed in the #1 category.

"Ensemble Techniques Monitoring" (Criterion Model #20) is another device that can be used for rehearsals. This device, like the "Rehearsal Procedures Monitoring," is a checklist type device to see what techniques are used and how often they are used.

To further investigate the workings of a rehearsal, one could make up eleven devices for further investigation into each of these areas given on the "Ensemble Techniques Monitoring." In the book, *How to Improve the High School Band Sound* (mentioned earlier), there is a "Check List of Key Problem Areas." That list gives some two hundred separate items that one can use for an in-depth diagnostic check while listening to a tape recording of a rehearsal. Since this list is so extensive, herein will be given only two examples of the kind of tool that can be drawn up.

TEACHER SELF-ANALYSIS

Self-analysis is a very difficult thing to do definitively and can be very deceiving. For some, their egos might not let them be honest, whereas others might become overly self-critical. There are, however, a few ways a self-analysis program can be done and be of great value as well as provide definitive information regarding the techniques that are being used.

One method is to go over a list of criteria and be as honest as possible without being super critical. Just reading a list of evaluative criteria can be very enlightening.

Another method is with the use of the video tape. Many times it is not only what is said, but how it is said. The body and facial movements that accompany verbal directions can be extremely important to how an idea is presented and how it is received by the students. In fact, seeing a video tape is much more revealing than even having a critical supervisor in the room with a long check list.

In his book, *Body Language* (New York: Pocket Books, 1984) Julius Fast has made a thorough investigation of how non-verbal movements reveal thought processes and how they send messages.

Still another method, other than a visit by a supervisor, would be to enlist the aid of a colleague. It can be extremely valuable to have a colleague observe a lesson and just generally discuss what happened, or provide him or her with a check list of some kind.

ON-THE-SPOT SELF-CHECK

It is possible to do an on-the-spot self-check. This only works in certain areas of teacher performance, however. Following is an example of an on-the-spot self-check that produces excellent results.

This band director (like many) acquired the habit of saying "OK" almost all the time. One day he kept two music stands in front of him. One was for his musical scores, the other for an 8½″ × 13″ legal pad. Each time he caught himself saying "OK" he put a check mark on the yellow pad. This was frequently done while the band was playing—the director conducting with one hand and making the check marks with the other. (One does not have to be ambidextrous to make a check mark.) Thirty-five check marks the first day showed the extent to which this had developed into a bad habit. Two days later the same thing was done again. The check marks were down to only fifteen—less than half the amount of the previous recording. The same procedure was repeated several more times. After three weeks of periodic checks, only one "OK" was recorded.

Other items that could be checked in this fashion would be things like always counting "one, two, ready, go." Frequently conductors get into the habit of tapping their baton on the music stand before starting. Some conductors fall into the habit of tapping the music stand to get the group to stop. One conductor that did not use a baton was observed clapping his hands just before the students were supposed to bring their instruments up to playing position.

A teacher should not use slang like "yep" or "uh huh" for "yes" and "nope" or "unnhun" for "no." This tendency could be the subject for an on-the-spot self-check.

Another habit one can fall into is saying "Let's go" each time the arms come up to prepare for the preparatory beat. Snapping the fingers to indicate tempo can also grow into an annoying habit. Some school music directors have even been observed snapping their fingers during concerts to indicate the tempo before they give the down-beat.

Some other things that might bare watching are: the number of times instructions are repeated; the number of times the voice has to be raised to overcome room noise, i.e., students talking; whether one bobs up and down by bending the knees on every beat; or whether one taps the foot while conducting.

Chapter 4

Facilities, Equipment, Materials, and Supplies

SEE: Page 97. Section VIII of Criterion Model #1: Criteria for Evaluating an Instrumental Music Department—Equipment.

AND: Page 99. Section IX of Criterion Model #1: Criteria for Evaluating an Instrumental Music Department—Supplies.

AND: Page 100. 1, Section X of Criterion Model #1: Criteria for Evaluating an Instrumental Music Department—Facilities.

The instrumental music department depends, as any part of the school, on the financial support given it by the school's administration for the purchase of the necessary equipment, materials, and supplies. The financial phase of the instrumental music program causes the greatest burden on the school district. Though proportionately it may not be much greater than any other subject, it does represent a considerable impact on the school's overall budget.

BIDS ON INSTRUMENTS

When a large number of instruments are to be purchased by a school district, the instruments usually have to be put out for bids. Usually, a document accompanies the announcement that bids are to be taken for various numbers and kinds of instruments. Included in the information sent out by the school district's business office should be some specifications, i.e., descriptions of the instruments that are to be purchased. A simplistic description might be something like this:

> fourteen B-flat soprano clarinets. Body: grenadilla wood. Mechanism: Boehm system with seventeen keys constructed of nickel-silver with matching mouthpiece. Case: sturdy, form-fitted with secure latches, handle, and hinging device.

Frequently, a particular make and model can be designated with the provision "or its equivalent."

Since bidding is meant to reduce the total cost on large quantity purchases, if care is not taken, the school can end up with inferior equipment. This can occur because the lowest bid is usually the one that is accepted. However, the lowest bid need not be taken if the specifications are such as to rule out cheap, inferior instruments. Besides giving complete specifications, it is possible to set up a check list for evaluating items that are proposed. Bidders are usually required (if it is a large quantity like ten to fourteen violins), to make available for examination a representative model of the item on which they are bidding. If the quality of an item is questionable, the criteria established will point up the fact that certain items should not be purchased.

"Criteria for Evaluating the Quality of a Clarinet" (Criterion Model #21) is a representative list of items. Only the highest quality clarinet would match this criteria. In fact, it is designed so that the clarinet from only one manufacturer will match it perfectly. This criteria is probably too stringent and specific for the kinds of instruments a school would normally purchase in any kind of quantity. It is only given as an example of the kinds of things that can be evaluated and specified.

This kind of criteria would have to be drawn up for each type of instrument being put out for bids. The information for specifications for various kinds of instruments can be acquired by writing to a manufacturer of the instruments desired. The degree of specificity needed would vary from one district and situation to another.

BUDGET CONSIDERATION

> SEE: Page 103. Section XI of Criterion Model #1: Criteria for Evaluating an Instrumental Music Program—Budget.

To what extent should the general taxpayers support the instrumental music program? The costs of various phases of the instrumental program can be borne in various ways. For example: If the marching band wishes to make a trip to some marching festival in a distant city, should the band raise its own monies or expect the school board to pay all expenses? If the orchestra would like to have uniforms, should the school board be expected to pay for them? Should the orchestra members and their parents be expected to raise their own funds for their uniforms as do many marching bands?

How much of the cost of various items of equipment used by the students should be borne by the school budget? Should the school's oboe player expect the school to purchase the reeds? Should the school's orchestra director have a supply of strings available to give to students free of charge? If the orchestra members get their strings free, should not the clarinet players be provided with free needs? Whereas it might seem only fair for the school to pay for the reeds of the baritone saxophone player since he is really a clarinetist, should not the bassoonist also have reeds provided free? This might then include that the band director should keep a supply of valve and slide oil for the brass players.

Should provisions be made for exceptionally talented students to take private lessons during the school day? Most students would be in class lessons or, by the time they get into high school, have to find some place outside the school to continue their study.

These questions can only be answered by music teachers within the context of individual situations. The philosophy of the teacher involved, however, will strongly influence the outcome of any situation. Is the instrumental program a "specialty" department, a general music program, or an entertainment medium for the school and community? The decision can only be made with a thorough knowledge of the attitudes of: the school administration (and not their public pronouncements), their relationships with the central administration and those individual's attitudes (also not their public pronouncements), and then, the board of education. The board of education can be quite easily manipulated by parents if the parents choose to take up the cause of the instrumental program. Local "Sports Boosters" (or by whatever name they call themselves) have taken up the cause of school sports across the country and acquired tremendous budgetary and support power.

Budget for Staffing

The following guidelines were used as the basis for arriving at an evaluation outcome for the budget allocations as they relate to the size of the teaching staff. The guidelines are those that were established by the New York State Department of Education.

1. The number of daily periods of classroom instruction should not exceed five.

2. In order that a sufficient amount of time is made available for this instruction, a minimum of one forty-minute class lesson per week is suggested.

3. One instructor can teach approximately 100 pupils in instrumental classes each week.

4. This may include giving individualized instruction, work with small groups (five to eight pupils maximum), and supervising participants in small ensemble and solo activities.

Using these guidelines, the following standards of relative time to pupil load are established:

1. A teacher should have five classes per day at forty minutes each.

2. If the classes should contain a minimum of five to eight students, the teacher would have twenty-five to a maximum of forty student contacts per day.

3. This would provide for 125 to a maximum of 200 student contacts per week.

Per-Pupil Cost

Frequently, budget-minded administrators can be impressed by the fact that the instrumental music program is not a very costly program per student. If other criteria can be used to show a good degree of accountability, it is effective to compare figures of the instrumental music department with other areas of instruction.

PER-PUPIL COST FORMULA

1. Enter the base salary(ies)   _____

2. Add the cost of teacher benefit   _____

3. This equals the total cost of salary(ies)   _____

4. Subtract the percent of time spent out of the area   _____

5. This equals pro-rated costs   _____

6. Add total budget for equipment, materials, and supplies   _____

7. This total is the cost of the program   _____

8. Divided by the number of students enrolled   _____

9. This equals the per-pupil costs   _____

Figure 4–1

It will be seen that the numbers of students enrolled in the music program have a direct bearing on the cost per pupil. The more students enrolled, the lower the cost. This, to be sure, is "playing the numbers game." Whereas the "numbers game" is not an educationally sound and justifiable way of looking at a program, it does play a major role in the educational system.

The "Per-Pupil Cost Formula" (see Figure 4–1) can be used for figuring out this aspect of the program.

When using this formula, the information for line number 2 (Add the cost of teacher benefits) can be gotten from the school's business office. That office can give the percentage of the base salary that is contributed by the school for fringe benefits like hospitalization, retirement, etc.

With regard to line number 4 (Subtract the percentage of time spent out of the area), this line is to differentiate between actual time spent in the area in question and time spent elsewhere. If the teacher spends time in study hall or teaching something besides the subject being checked, this time is deducted from the salary figure. For example, if the figure is to indicate the cost of the high school band and the teacher spends half of his day teaching in the elementary school, then the figure would be 50 percent. If the teacher has hall duty five times a week, then the formula would be one-seventh. This figure would be arrived at as follows:

> If there are eight periods a day with one off for lunch, then there would be thirty-five teaching periods per week. Five of those periods are devoted to non-music duties. Thus, 5/35 of the salary is not devoted to teaching the band—the figure gets reduced by 1/7.

Chapter 5

Program Outcomes

This chapter deals with items that will show the successes or the needs that the department might have. They include such items as:

Music Literacy Survey Outcomes

Kwalwasser-Ruch Test Outcomes

Criteria for Evaluating an
Instrumental Music Department—
Composite Outcomes

Watkins-Farnum Outcomes

Composite Values of Grade vs.
Rating System (C. V. D. L.)

Any standardized test can be made into a program outcome. The "Music Literacy Survey" is an excellent vehicle to use as a program outcome indicator.* This would be especially good if a school administrator or some of the parents are knowledgeable about the more progressive field of music education. (As discussed earlier, most parents and administrators are only interested in the students' public performance image.)

Another excellent vehicle is the Kwalwasser-Ruch Test Outcome (see Figure 5–1). By keeping records of these tests over a period of years, an idea can be

*A full discussion of the "Music Literacy Survey Outcomes" is given in *Instrumental Music Evaluation Kit* by Russell A. Pizer (West Nyack, NY: Parker Publishing, 1987). It also discusses methods of charting outcomes.

KWALWASSER-RUCH TEST OF THEORETICAL MUSICAL KNOWLEDGE

Chart shows the number of tests taken and grades received within various percentiles

Grade 8 — Jennsong Elementary Orchestra

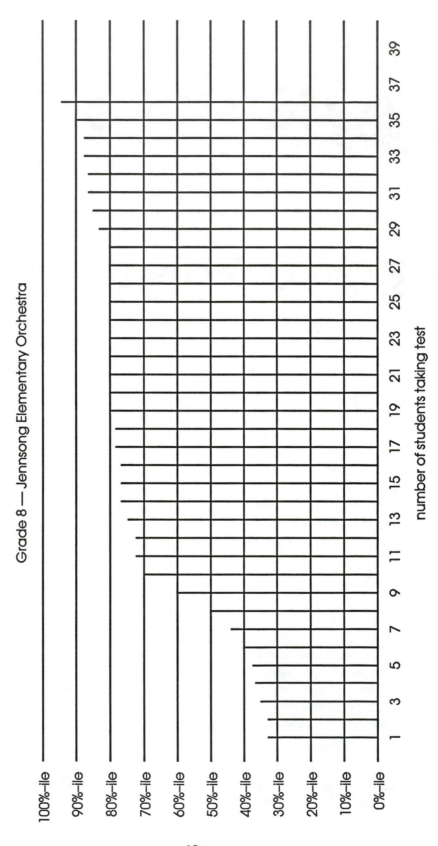

number of students taking test

Figure 5–1

acquired as to how the program is providing technical information to the students.

EVALUATIVE CRITERIA OUTCOMES

There are forms provided for arriving at what will be a single figure showing the outcome of all the "Criteria for Evaluating an Instrumental Music Department" (Criterion Model #1) as well as various divisions within the department. The "Work Sheets" will allow for an accumulation of individual ratings in each of the sub-categories. The "Composite Outcome" gives a single, overall look at the program on a graph. The work sheet provides page numbers where each of the items of the Criteria may be located.

Depending on the situation, it may be valuable to abstract items from various areas of the Criteria and make a composite picture of, for example, just the high school program, or just the district's orchestra program. In this case, the Criteria for the areas apropos to that part of the program would be used. Provided also is a work sheet for evaluating just the band and just the orchestra programs by themselves. (See "Outcomes for Evaluation of the Band Program—Work Sheet" - page 58, and "Outcomes for the Evaluation of the Orchestra Program—Work Sheet" - page 61.) For the final outcome, however, both would use the "Total Outcomes" and be charted on the "Composite Outcomes."

WATKINS-FARNUM BAROMETER

Though the *Watkins-Farnum Performance Scale* and the *Watkins String Scale* are devices for testing individual students, they also can be used as a means of evaluating the program as a whole. For a complete description of these two vehicles see: *Instrumental Music Evaluation Kit*. (West Nyack, NY: Parker Pub. Co., 1987.)

For use in a program of evaluation, a record can be made of the total number of errors made by all the instrumentalists in the program. The type of errors would be plotted on a graph like that shown as "W-F Outcomes" (see Figure 5-2). By observing which areas of performance have the most number of errors, one could see in which area of instruction more emphasis should be made. In the illustration given (Figure 5-2), pitch and time errors were the most numerous.

Another means of using the *Watkins-Farnum Performance Scale* and the *Farnum String Scale* outcomes would be to prepare statistics for the "Watkins-Farnum Performance Scale Barometer" (See Figure 5-3) and a similar chart for the "Farnum String Scale." In this way, one may find the instrumental processes are actually improving the performance of the individuals within the program from year to year. In the illustration given (see Figure 5-3), the playing quality of the organization as a whole is just above the statistical averages.

W-F OUTCOMES

number and percentage of errors by type of error

DATE _____

ERRORS	Pitch	Time	Slur	Rest	Tempo	Repeats	Expression
# of errors:	139	119	64	35	23	12	32
% of errors:	48%	41%	22%	12%	8%	4%	11%

Figure 5–2

WATKINS-FARNUM PERFORMANCE SCALE BAROMETER

DATE_____

SCORE

X-VILLE SCHOOL DISTRICT'S
OUTCOMES

SOLID LINE = STATISTICAL
AVERAGES

BROKEN LINE = SCHOOL
DISTRICT'S AVERAGES

ISOLATED DOTS = HIGHEST
SCORE ACHIEVED BY AN
INDIVIDUAL

YEARS STUDIED:	1	2	3	4	5	6
Statistical averages:	32	52	63	76	83	86
School district's averages:	35	56	67	82	91	95
Score points above or below statistical averages:	+3	+4	+4	+6	+8	+9

Figure 5–3

C. V. D. L.

Though the Composite Values of Grade vs. Rating system (C.V.D.L.) is established for making the ratings received by various organizations and soloists at the state-run competition-festivals into a simple letter grade which could be used on a school report card, it can also be used to indicate overall program achievements. The C.V.D.L. system would only give indicators of student performance abilities. It would not give any definitive aid to the teacher to upgrade his teaching. It could, however, show trends over a period of time.

C.V.D.L. is the method by which the ratings received by various individuals and organizations participating in music competition-festivals can be reduced to a grade that might be entered on a hypothetical instrumental music program report card.

A total discussion of C.V.D.L. is contained in *Instrumental Music Evaluation Kit*. Specifically, C.V.D.L. stands for: "composite value of the degree of technical and musical difficulty of a musical composition performed at a competition-festival as it relates to the performance proficiency level awarded by the adjudicator(s)." Additionally, the grade (*DoD* - Degree of Difficulty) and its relation to the rating (*LoPP* - Level of Performance Proficiency) is correlated to the type of school from which the student or ensemble comes. This correlation is made by consulting the C.V.D.L. Equalization Charts (See Appendix B). These C.V.D.L. charts translate the grade (*DoD*) into a single figure representing a desired level of proficiency in technical and musical achievement based on the level in school, with 100 being a perfect score at certain levels. There is a separate chart for grade-rating for high school, middle school, junior high, and various types of elementary schools.

The equalization charts (Appendix B) are graduated so that students in grades 11 and 12 enter *DoD*-6 and receive a *LoPP* of A+ in order to receive a C.V.D.L. of 100 (See Chart VI). A middle school student need only enter *DoD*-4 and receive an A+ to acquire a C.V.D.L. of 100 (See Chart IVa). If a soloist is in the 10th grade and finds it necessary to enter *DoD*-4, the highest C.V.D.L. he can receive is 95 (See Chart IV). If he should enter a grade level too high for his requisite abilities, he is indirectly penalized. Whereas he might get an *A* by entering *DoD*-4, he may only receive a *LoPP-C* in *DoD*-6. The C.V.D.L. for *A* in *DoD*-4 is 92. The C.V.D.L. for a *LoPP-C* in *DoD*-5 is 77 (See Chart V).

Some of the uses of the C.V.D.L regarding the department as a whole is to translate the band's or orchestra's rating (*LoPP*) into a simple C.V.D.L. figure. For example: a high school group that enters *DoD*-5 and receives a *LoPP-A*, receives a "program-report-card-grade" of 92.

If the group in previous years has entered a lower *DoD* and got *LoPP*s of *A*s and/or *B*s, it would be valuable for the program to make up a chart showing the differences. The "High School Orchestra C.V.D.L. Record" (see Figure 5-4) shows a hypothetical C.V.D.L. record.

An average of all the soloists that entered the competition-festival could be made up, showing again the improvement or decline over previous years.

HIGH SCHOOL ORCHESTRA C.V.D.L. RECORD

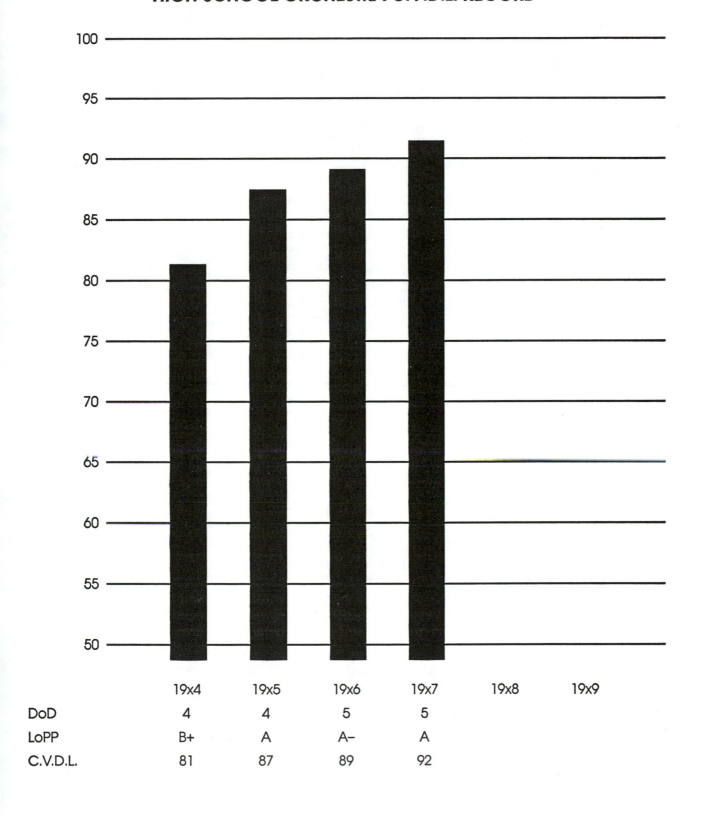

	19x4	19x5	19x6	19x7	19x8	19x9
DoD	4	4	5	5		
LoPP	B+	A	A–	A		
C.V.D.L.	81	87	89	92		

Figure 5–4

45

Raceville School District's C.V.D.L. Summary
for the
19XX Competition-Festival

With ratio to school enrollments

	Soloists			
R.H.S. Band	Total C.V.D.L.	1428		
	Average C.V.D.L. (17 involved)		85	
	Ratio to school enrollment (2792)			.51
R.H.S. Chorus	Total C.V.D.L.	1317		
	Average C.V.D.L. (17 involved)		77	
	Ratio to school enrollment (2792)			.41
Janup School Band	Total C.V.D.L.	866		
	Average C.V.D.L. (9 involved)		97	
	Ratio to school enrollment (786)			1.10
Bevann School Band	Total C.V.D.L.	100		
	Average C.V.D.L. (1 involved)		100	
	Ratio to school enrollment (711)			.14
	Small ensembles			
R.H.S. Band	Total C.V.D.L.	404		
	Average C.V.D.L. (5 ensembles)		81	
	Ratio to school enrollment (2792)			.14
R.H.S. Chorus	Total C.V.D.L.	562		
	Average C.V.D.L. (7 ensembles)		80	
	Ratio to school enrollment (2791)			.20
Bevann School Band	Total C.V.D.L.	270		
	Average C.V.D.L. (3 ensembles)		90	
	Ratio to school enrollment (711)			.39

Figure 5–5

An average C.V.D.L. received by small ensembles entered in the competition-festivals would also make interesting departmental statistics.

As an adjunct to the basic C.V.D.L. figure, a ratio to school enrollment can be shown. This is done by adding together all the C.V.D.L. figures of the students who played solos and dividing this by the entire school enrollment. For example, if the school enrollment is 750 and the total C.V.D.L. figure is 860, the ratio of C.V.D.L. to school enrollment would be 1:10. In succeeding years if the individual ratings go up as well as the number of students participating, the ratio could be 1:18 (i.e., 780 enrollment vs. C.V.D.L. total of 920). In showing these figures, it

Enrollment Figures

*Percentages of students enrolled in the instrumental music
program in Raceville Public Schools*

	School enrollment 4/1/XX	Numbers of students enrolled in instru. music	Percentage of enrollment
North Middle School	786	111	14.3%
South Middle School	711	71	10.1%
Jason West	343	41	12.0%
Washington	302	33	11.0%
Babbon	429	59	13.7%
Jennifore	455	70	15.3%
Trace	315	20	6.3%
Oneida	543	66	12.1%
Jammore	399	92*	23.0%
Robrus	192	9	4.1%
TOTALS	4495	572	12.2%

*This includes a Flutophone class

Raceville High School	2792	93	3.3%

Staffing assignment proportions	Elementary	Middle	High School
J. Janup	10/10	0	0
T. Bell	0	0	10/10
W. Watson	1/10	6/10	3/10
A. Vail	10/10	0	0
K. Gayle	2/10	8/10	0
P. Lessur	4/10	6/10	3/10
R. Ingersol	4/10	6/10	0

Figure 5–6

means that not only the degree of participation is going up, but the individual
abilities are improving.

Above are some examples of how these figures can be shown and reported.
(See Figure 5–5.)

The report showing "Enrollment Figures" (see Figure 5–6) gives an overall
picture of the attraction students have to the program. The "Staffing Assignment
Proportions" at the bottom is figured by half days, i.e., there are ten half days
during the week. If a teacher spends one day at one school, say Jane Jennifore

**C.V.D.L. Summary
for
19XX Competition-Festival**

Major ensembles	R.H.S. Band	88
	R.H.S. Mixed Chorus	73
	R.H.S. Orchestra	83
	North Jr. High School Band	92
Soloists	R.H.S. Band members	85
	R.H.S. Orchestra members	92
	North Jr. High School Band members	97
	South Jr. High School Band members (only 1 entered)	100
Small ensembles	R.H.S. Band Members	81
	R.H.S. Orchestra members	94
	South Jr. High School Band members	90

Figure 5–7

Elementary School, the proportion would be 2/10 for that particular school. If he or she spends only half a day there, the proportion would be 1/10. And, if he or she spends all day Monday, Wednesday, and Friday at that school, the proportion would be 6/10.

The C.V.D.L. Summary for "19XX N.Y.S.S.M.A. Competition Festival" (see Figure 5–7) shows that the C.V.D.L. can also be used in connection with choirs and vocal soloists.

Part 2

The Criteria

CRITERION MODEL #1

CRITERIA FOR EVALUATING AN INSTRUMENTAL MUSIC PROGRAM*

The criteria given in the checklists that follow are designed for an urban school system where several schools are involved and there is at least one non-teaching music administrator. However, as will be seen through the use of one evaluative value (the letter "N") the criteria can be used even in the smallest school system or an individual school.

These criteria can give a clear picture of offerings in instrumental music. The outcomes can be charted and reduced to a simple four-point outcome.

The evaluation process is as follows:

Step 1

Evaluate each item in the criteria as follows:

E — if the provision or condition is made extensively (A)
S — if the provision or condition is made to some extent (B)
L — if the provision or condition is limited (C)
V — if the provision or condition is very limited (D)
M — if the provision or condition is missing and needed (F)
N — if the provision or condition does not apply or is not necessarily desirable

The letters at the left (E S L V M N) are to be placed on the lines provided with each criteria item. The letters at the right (A B C D F) are given to show the relationship between the letters of evaluation and the normal letter-grading system.

Step 2

After completing the evaluation of each item in the criteria, count the number of letters used. Count all the letters except *N*, as these provisions are considered as not desirable or do not apply.

*© 1966 by The Instrumentalist Co. Reprinted by permission from *The Instrumentalist*, January 1966. Subscriptions are available from The Instrumentalist Co., 200 Northfield Road, Northfield, Illinois, USA.

Step 3

Add the values of each letter used as follows:

$$E = 4, S = 3, L = 2, V = 1, M = 0$$

Step 4

Divide the total number of letters used in Step 2 into the total letter values from Step 3.

Step 5

Enter the numerical scores on the chart of "Composite Outcomes." Average the major subsections to arrive at a single value for each roman numeraled section.

Step 6

Enter the averages of each roman numeraled section on the "Total Outcomes" sheet, then average these figures for a "Final Outcome."

Step 7

To determine the strength or weakness of the program in verbal values, the following correlations are made:

> 3.3 to 4.0 = excellent
> 2.5 to 3.2 = very good
> 1.7 to 2.4 = good
> 0.9 to 1.6 = fair
> 0.0 to 0.8 = poor

COMPOSITE OUTCOMES

I. ADMINISTRATION

    A. Guidance   ——

    B. Supervision of personnel   ——

    C. Teacher training and guidance   ——

    D. Promotional activities   ——

                                      OUTCOME: ——

II. CURRICULUM

    A. General   ——

    B. Primary   ——

    C. Pre-band   ——

    D. Elementary   ——

    E. Junior High   ——

    F. High School   ——

                OUTCOME: ——

III. PROGRAM

    A. Primary   ——

    B. Pre-band   ——

    C. Exploratory Class   ——

    D. Rental program—school owned instruments   ——

    E. Rental program—from a commercial company   ——

    F. Elementary   ——

    G. Junior High   ——

    H. High School   ——

    J. Band Instrumentation   ——

    K. Orchestra Instrumentation   ——

    L. Summer Program   ——

    M. High School Stage Band   ——

                OUTCOME: ——

IV. PERFORMANCES

A. Elementary Band   _____

B. Elementary Orchestra   _____

C. Junior High Band   _____

D. Junior High Orchestra   _____

E. High School Band   _____

F. High School Orchestra   _____

OUTCOME: _____

V. SCHEDULING

A. Administrative   _____

B. Pre-band   _____

C. Elementary   _____

D. Junior High   _____

E. High School   _____

OUTCOME: _____

VI. EQUIPMENT

A. Equipment Management   _____

B. General Equipment—Elementary   _____

C. General Equipment—Junior High   _____

D. General Equipment—High School   _____

E. Primary Instruments   _____

F. Elementary Instruments   _____

G. Junior High Instruments   _____

H. High School Instruments   _____

J. Marching Band Instruments   _____

K. Condition of Instruments   _____

L. Marching Band Equipment   _____

OUTCOME: _____

VII. MATERIALS AND SUPPLIES

A. Elementary   _____

B. Junior High   _____

C. High School   _____

OUTCOME: _____

VIII. FACILITIES

Physical setup

A. Elementary Band   ———
B. Elementary Orchestra   ———
C. Junior High Band   ———
D. Junior High Orchestra   ———
E. High School Band   ———
F. High School Orchestra   ———
G. Marching Band   ———

Storage

H. Elementary Band   ———
J. Elementary Orchestra   ———
K. Junior High Band   ———
L. Junior High Orchestra   ———
M. High School Band   ———
N. High School Orchestra   ———

                                 OUTCOME: ———

IX. BUDGET

A. Staffing   ———
B. Administration of   ———
C. Equipment   ———
D. Materials and Supplies   ———
E. Activities and Fees   ———
F. Distribution of Funds   ———

                                 OUTCOME: ———

TOTAL OUTCOMES

I. ADMINISTRATIVE   ————

II. CURRICULUM   ————

III. PROGRAM   ————

IV. PERFORMANCE   ————

V. SCHEDULING   ————

VI. EQUIPMENT   ————

VII. MATERIALS AND SUPPLIES   ————

VIII. FACILITIES   ————

IX. BUDGET   ————

The average of I through IX becomes the final outcome for the entire department   ————

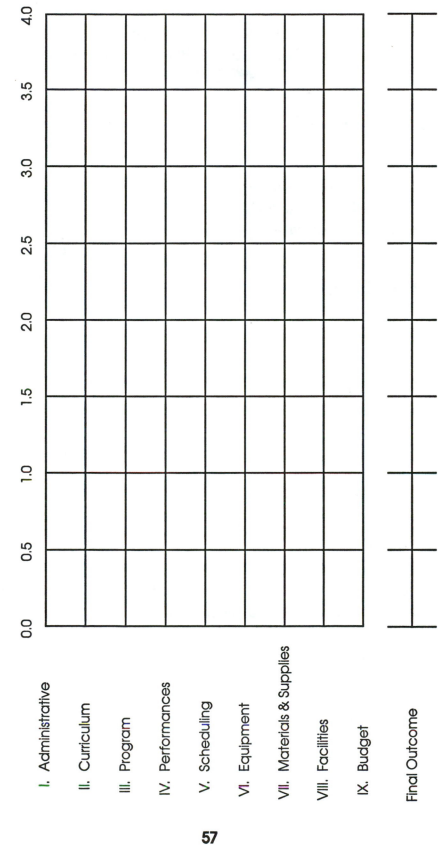

COMPOSITE OUTCOMES

I. Administrative

II. Curriculum

III. Program

IV. Performances

V. Scheduling

VI. Equipment

VII. Materials & Supplies

VIII. Facilities

IX. Budget

Final Outcome

Outcomes for the
EVALUATION OF THE BAND PROGRAM
WORK SHEET

I. ADMINISTRATION

    A. Guidance   _____
    B. Supervision of Personnel   _____
    C. Teacher Training and Guidance   _____
    D. Promotional Activities   _____

                              OUTCOME: _____

II. CURRICULUM

    A. General   _____
    B. Primary   _____
    C. Pre-band   _____
    D. Elementary   _____
    E. Junior High   _____
    F. High School   _____

                              OUTCOME: _____

III. PROGRAM

    A. Primary   _____
    B. Pre-band   _____
    C. Exploratory Class   _____
    D. Rental Program—school-owned instruments   _____
    E. Rental Program—from a commercial company   _____
    F. Elementary   _____
    G. Junior High   _____
    H. High School   _____
    J. Band Instrumentation   _____
    K. Summer Program   _____
    L. High School Stage Band   _____

                              OUTCOME: _____

IV. PERFORMANCE

    A. Elementary Band   _____

    B. Junior High Band   _____

    C. High School Band   _____

                                OUTCOME: _____

V. SCHEDULING

    A. Administrative   _____

    B. Pre-band   _____

    C. Elementary   _____

    D. Junior High   _____

    E. High School   _____

                                OUTCOME: _____

VI. EQUIPMENT

    A. Equipment Management   _____

    B. General Equipment—Elementary   _____

    C. General Equipment—Junior High   _____

    D. General Equipment—High School   _____

    E. Primary Instruments   _____

    F. Elementary Instruments   _____

    G. Junior High Instruments   _____

    H. High School Instruments   _____

    J. Marching Band Instruments   _____

    K. Condition of Instruments   _____

    L. Marching Band Equipment   _____

                                OUTCOME: _____

VII. MATERIALS & SUPPLIES

    A. Elementary   _____

    B. Junior high   _____

    C. High School   _____

                                OUTCOME: _____

VIII. FACILITIES

Physical setup

A. Elementary Band   _____
B. Junior High Band   _____
C. High School Band   _____
D. Marching Band   _____

Storage

E. Elementary Band   _____
F. Junior High Band   _____
G. High School Band   _____

                                        OUTCOME: _____

IX. BUDGET

A. Staffing   _____
B. Administration   _____
C. Equipment   _____
D. Materials and Supplies   _____
E. Activities and Fees   _____
F. Distribution of Funds   _____

                                        OUTCOME: _____

Outcomes for the
EVALUATION OF THE ORCHESTRA PROGRAM
WORK SHEET

I. ADMINISTRATION

   A. Guidance _____

   B. Supervision of Personnel _____

   C. Teacher Training and Guidance _____

   D. Promotional Activities _____

                               OUTCOME: ____

II. CURRICULUM

   A. General _____

   B. Primary _____

   C. Elementary _____

   D. Junior High _____

   E. High School _____

                               OUTCOME: ____

III. PROGRAM

   A. Primary _____

   B. Rental Program—school-owned instruments _____

   C. Rental Program—from a commercial company _____

   D. Elementary _____

   E. Junior High _____

   F. High School _____

   G. Instrumentation _____

   H. Summer Program _____

                               OUTCOME: ____

IV. PERFORMANCE

   A. Elementary Orchestra _____

   B. Junior High Orchestra _____

   C. High School Orchestra _____

                               OUTCOME: ____

V. SCHEDULING

    A. Administrative   _____

    B. Elementary   _____

    C. Junior High   _____

    D. High School   _____

                    OUTCOME: _____

VI. EQUIPMENT

    A. Equipment Management   _____

    B. General Equipment—Elementary   _____

    C. General Equipment—Junior High   _____

    D. General Equipment—High School   _____

    E. Primary Instruments   _____

    F. Elementary Instruments   _____

    G. Junior High Instruments   _____

    H. High School Instruments   _____

                    OUTCOME: _____

VII. MATERIALS & SUPPLIES

    A. Elementary   _____

    B. Junior high   _____

    C. High school   _____

                    OUTCOME: _____

VIII. FACILITIES

Physical setup

    A. Elementary Orchestra   _____

    B. Junior High Orchestra   _____

    C. High School Orchestra   _____

Storage

    D. Elementary Orchestra   _____

    E. Junior High Orchestra   _____

    F. High School Orchestra   _____

                    OUTCOME: _____

IX. BUDGET

A. Staffing   ———

B. Administration of   ———

C. Equipment   ———

D. Materials and Supplies   ———

E. Activities and Fees   ———

F. Distribution of Funds   ———

OUTCOME: ———

NOTE: For Total Outcomes and Composite Outcomes use page 56.

SECTION I—THE ADMINISTRATOR

Item A—Administrative Guidance

_____ 1. Sees that the first emphasis is placed on fine classroom teaching rather than the mere preparation of specialized groups for the giving of concerts, preparation for festivals, contests, etc.

_____ 2. Guides the formulation of the music education philosophy and statement of aims.

_____ 3. Determines and implements the philosophy and school policy regarding music.

_____ 4. Directs needed studies and investigations, devises and gathers records, and evaluates and reports.

_____ 5. Constantly seeks new truths, continually evaluates aims and objectives, and is philosophic.

_____ 6. Works toward common ends and works with teachers toward the solution of mutual problems.

_____ 7. Applies the scientific method to the study of teaching process, seeks proof as to its own accomplishments, and encourages experimentation under proper control.

_____ 8. Helps teachers secure effective working knowledge of the tools of teaching, the courses of study, standard tests, instructional materials, and equipment, and seeks to improve these tools and coordinate them with theory and practice.

SECTION I—THE ADMINISTRATOR

Item B—Supervision of Personnel

_____ 1. Selects and recommends competent teachers for employment.

_____ 2. Organizes the music teaching staff to assure smooth functioning.

_____ 3. Establishes and maintains a good attitude toward music on the part of the teaching staff.

_____ 4. Unifies and vitalizes the personnel in the program.

_____ 5. Sees that rhythm band activities are under the direction of a well-informed person.

_____ 6. Provides for the pre-band class of instruction under the direction of a specialist in instrumental music.

_____ 7. Gives classroom teachers training in the use of the pre-band instruments.

_____ 8. Encourages classroom teachers to assist this pre-band training by giving additional materials as a reward for good work completed in other fields.

_____ 9. Observes teaching for purposes of rating and counseling.

SECTION I—THE ADMINISTRATOR

Item C—Teacher Training and Guidance

_____ 1. Holds individual and group conferences with teachers for the purpose of discussing music teaching problems.

_____ 2. Conducts in-service music classes for teachers.

_____ 3. Arranges for extension classes.

_____ 4. Gives demonstration lessons.

_____ 5. Arranges for visitation to other schools.

_____ 6. Carries desirable music-teaching procedures from one school to another.

_____ 7. Assists with the planning and preparation of special music programs.

_____ 8. Provides opportunities for teachers to develop themselves musically and encourages them to do so through private study and/or participation in musical activities.

_____ 9. Stimulates attendance to concerts.

_____ 10. Calls attention to and encourages listening to desirable radio and television programs.

_____ 11. Makes professional books and magazines easily available and calls attention to especially helpful writings.

_____ 12. Sets up and administers tests to measure the effectiveness of music instruction and interprets results of teaching procedures.

_____ 13. Evaluates and selects textbooks, music, and equipment.

_____ 14. Covers music education or general professional literature for help on problems related to teaching.

_____ 15. Assists in the assembling of curriculum materials.

_____ 16. Prepares courses of study.

SECTION I—THE ADMINISTRATOR

Item D—Promotional Activities

_____ 1. Establishes the director(s) as musical leader(s) inside and outside the school.

_____ 2. Creates effective contacts between the director(s) and various other school departments.

_____ 3. Develops inter-school music activities.

_____ 4. Develops programs that feature several different school music departments.

_____ 5. Creates cooperation with other departments in order to minimize the conflict between instrumental schedules and the general school program.

_____ 6. Stresses to the organizations' members their duty to maintain a high scholastic standing.

_____ 7. Seeks out special ways in which to help other school departments.

_____ 8. Shares in other school functions by being alert to educational programs of interest to other teachers.

_____ 9. Creates effective contact between the director(s) and school authorities.

_____ 10. Notifies school authorities of special music activities.

_____ 11. Keeps school authorities informed of any special honors received by the organization and its members.

_____ 12. Informs school board members of the value of music training and its importance to the school and community.

_____ 13. Provides information to the board members from the director(s), parents, and friends of the music program.

_____ 14. Assures that contact is created between the director(s) and parents of children participating in the instrumental organizations.

_____ 15. Helps director(s) keep parents informed of their child's music progress by personal contact and/or reports in card or letter form.

_____ 16. Helps director(s) keep parents informed of the department's aims and objectives.

_____ 17. Helps director(s) keep parents informed of the activities of the musical organizations.

_____ 18. Retains effective contact between the director(s) and civic groups.

_____ 19. Maintains contact with community groups that would be interested in musical programs.

_____ 20. Provides musical organizations to aid in promoting civic and charitable programs.

_____ 21. Provides assistance in the planning of such civic events as parades, formal dedications, public festivals, etc.

_____ 22. Assists churches by providing instrumental music for services and special programs.

_____ 23. Keeps the newspapers informed as to the activities of the department and provides articles and pictures.

_____ 24. Provides special programs periodically for radio and/or television broadcasts.

_____ 25. Provides tapes and films of contests, festivals, and concerts for presentation over radio and/or television.

_____ 26. Purchases space in the newspaper, as well as radio and television time, for announcements of concerts and special events.

SECTION II—THE CURRICULUM

Item A—General Considerations

_____ 1. The administrator helps formulate, revise, and apply the music curriculum.

_____ 2. The administrator helps facilitate interchange of ideas regarding a well-balanced vocal and instrumental curriculum on the primary, elementary, and secondary levels.

_____ 3. The administrator helps promote a close relationship between music and other subjects.

_____ 4. Appreciation of instrumental music is given to general music classes through films and instrumental demonstrations.

_____ 5. All children are given some formal type of instruction in rules of concert conduct.

_____ 6. Outside groups such as bands, chamber music groups, orchestras, and soloists appear at school assemblies periodically.

_____ 7. All musical performances for and about the school are supervised by music department personnel.

_____ 8. The general music class often includes recordings and information about instrumental music.

SECTION II—THE CURRICULUM

Item B—Primary Curriculum

_____ 1. Ample opportunity is given for music classes to hear music of the great orchestras, bands, and ensembles.

_____ 2. Students are familiar with such musical compositions as symphonies, suites, overtures, etc.

_____ 3. The classes in general music learn about the various instruments of the band and orchestra.

———— 4. The primary students can differentiate between wind, string, and percussion instruments.

———— 5. The primary students can name the various parts of the instruments like the valve, reed, mouthpiece, finger board, etc.

———— 6. Sets of books like *Musical Books for Young People* compiled by Robert W. Surplus (Minneapolis: Lerner, 1963) are a regular part of the instrumental program.

———— 7. The knowledge of reading rhythm is applied through the use of rhythm band instrument classes.

———— 8. The knowledge of reading music (via scales) is applied through the use of keyboard experiences.

———— 9. Extensive work is done in the area of solfeggio.

SECTION II—THE CURRICULUM

Item C—Pre-Band Curriculum

———— 1. The instruction books for the pre-band program contain a logical approach to reading music.

———— 2. Instruction books are selected to suit the types of children in various schools/classes.

———— 3. Through this course children are able to read music at sight.

———— 4. Children learn finger dexterity and the use of the tongue for executing rhythmic figures.

———— 5. Fundamental rudiments of music are included as a part of the pre-band class work.

———— 6. A part of each class is used to introduce the children to the instruments they may play in the future and the technical problems they may encounter on both band and orchestra instruments.

———— 7. At the conclusion of the program, tests such as the Music Guidance Survey are given as a means of pointing out those children with musical ability who should be selected to continue on into beginning instrumental classes.

SECTION II—THE CURRICULUM

Item D—Elementary Curriculum

———— 1. The beginning instrumental curriculum is established in such a way as to lay a firm foundation of position, posture, breathing/bowing, tone production, articulation, rhythm, intonation, and technic.

_____ 2. A curriculum of successive instruction books is established to regulate student advancement.

_____ 3. A repertory list of elementary solos of different degrees of difficulty is established.

_____ 4. Materials are provided for instruction in the care of instruments.

_____ 5. Correct illustrations of fundamental posture are included in the instruction books or are given as supplementary material.

_____ 6. Correct illustrations of fundamental embouchure/bow positions are included in the instruction books or are given as supplementary material.

_____ 7. Complete fingering charts are included in the instruction books or are given as supplementary material.

_____ 8. Technical problems are introduced logically and functionally.

_____ 9. A step-by-step process of assembling instruments is included in the instruction books or is provided as supplementary material.

_____ 10. Formalized instruction is provided in methods of practicing.

SECTION II—THE CURRICULUM

Item E—Junior High School Curriculum

_____ 1. The curriculum is established in such a way as to continue development of such fundamentals as posture, breathing/bowing, tone production, articulation, rhythm, intonation, and technic.

_____ 2. Formalized instruction is provided in methods of practicing.

_____ 3. The instruction book contains a logical approach to further develop the student's musicianship and understanding of fine instrumental performance.

_____ 4. Instruction books with progressively more difficult technical exercises are used to continue the development of instrumental facility.

_____ 5. A definite class routine is established so students learn proper methods of phrasing, playing with expression, and proper musical styles.

_____ 6. A firm foundation of musical knowledge is built through the performance and use of scales, scale patterns, and scale exercises.

_____ 7. Solo playing is stressed as a means to understand the use of the instrument and lay a foundation for an appreciation of fine professional, artistic performances.

_____ 8. Basic theory is introduced through scale exercises and patterns.

_____ 9. Overall knowledge of musical forms is developed through the analysis of music used in lessons and band/orchestra rehearsals.

_____ 10. A program is established so students learn the musical terminology that is connected with the compositions they perform.

_____ 11. A program is established to teach students how to listen to and understand great works of music performed by the best bands and orchestras of our day.

_____ 12. The music selected for performances by the band/orchestra is specifically designed to develop technical skills, performance abilities, musical knowledge, and musical understanding.

_____ 13. The music selected for performances by the band/orchestra is not only studied for the technical aspects, but also for the musical background, form, and style.

_____ 14. The music that is offered for performances by the band/orchestra is considered for its balance of various styles and historical periods.

SECTION II—THE CURRICULUM

Item F—High School Curriculum

_____ 1. The curriculum offerings consist of specifically selected materials to develop technical skills, performance abilities, and musical knowledge and understanding.

_____ 2. The materials selected for performances by the band/orchestra are aimed at improving the depth of students' knowledge and understanding of music as a fine art.

_____ 3. The music that is offered for performances by the band/orchestra is considered for its balance of various styles and historical periods.

_____ 4. The music selected for performances by the band/orchestra is not only studied from the technical aspects but from its musical background, form, and style as well.

_____ 5. The curriculum is established so there is a continued development of individual technical skills.

_____ 6. Instruction books are used to continue the development of students' musicianship and understanding of fine instrumental performances.

_____ 7. Instructional books with progressively more difficult technical exercises are an integral part of the program.

_____ 8. A definite routine is established for technic lessons so students learn proper methods of phrasing, playing with expression, and musical styles.

_____ 9. Formalized instruction is provided in methods of practicing.

_____ 10. A firm foundation of musical knowledge is built through the performance and use of scales, scale patterns, and scale exercises.

_____ 11. Solo playing is stressed as a means of understanding the use of the instrument and laying a foundation to appreciate and understand fine professional performance.

_____ 12. A formal list of solo materials is established which will progressively improve the students' solo performance abilities and understanding of this facet of musical performance.

_____ 13. Basic theory is introduced through some formalized instructional approach.

_____ 14. Overall knowledge of musical forms is developed through some formalized instructional approach.

_____ 15. A program is established to teach students the musical terminology that is connected with the compositions they are performing.

_____ 16. A program is established to teach students to listen to and understand great works of music as performed by the best bands, orchestras, soloists, and chamber groups of our day.

SECTION III—THE PROGRAM

Item A—Primary Grade Program

_____ 1. Children in the primary grades are given instruction in rhythm band instruments.

_____ 2. A portion of the general music class is devoted to listening to and constructively talking about instrumental music.

_____ 3. Audio equipment is provided in every classroom.

_____ 4. The children are made instrument-conscious by hearing and seeing older children play their instruments for classes.

_____ 5. Art classes encourage children to draw pictures of instrumentalists playing clarinets, trumpets, violins, drums, etc.

_____ 6. Some keyboard experience is given.

_____ 7. There are sufficient numbers of good quality recordings to introduce the children to symphonic literature that they can understand.

SECTION III—THE PROGRAM

Item B—Pre-Band Program

_____ 1. Pre-band instrumental instruction is given to all 4th graders.

_____ 2. The class is designed to allow the instrumental music teachers to become acquainted with the personalities of the children and observe their personal traits.

_____ 3. The class is designed to give the children a pleasant experience in performing instrumental music.

_____ 4. The class is designed to give the children an enjoyable musical experience that develops their ability to sight-read music.

_____ 5. The class is used primarily to teach music through the medium of an easily playable instrument, not to recruit for the band or orchestra.

_____ 6. To stimulate interest in the instrumental program, films such as "Toot, Whistle, Plunk, and Boom," "Introducing the Woodwinds," etc., are shown on a regular basis.

_____ 7. Brochures of information like "Your Child Is Musical," by Sigmund Spaeth and "The Complete Education Includes Music," by the American Music Conference are sent home periodically.

_____ 8. Parents are kept informed of the children's progress through periodic reports.

_____ 9. These reports contain such information as work habits, cooperation, courtesy, initiative, and musicianship.

SECTION III—THE PROGRAM

Item C—Exploratory Classes

_____ 1. Exploratory classes are given on the instruments that are available in the beginning band and orchestra program.

_____ 2. These classes are open to selected students who have shown interest in learning to play an instrument.

_____ 3. Exploratory classes meet on a regular basis with specialists on the various instruments.

_____ 4. The children are given the opportunity of playing any instrument of their choice.

_____ 5. The students are encouraged to try all the instruments that are available.

_____ 6. An accurate record is kept of a child's success on each instrument for counseling purposes once the exploratory class has concluded.

_____ 7. Results of the exploratory class are used for final selection of instruments for the beginning band and orchestra program.

SECTION III—THE PROGRAM

Item D—Instrument Rental Program—School-Owned Instruments

_____ 1. Sufficient rental is charged to keep all instruments in excellent working condition.

_____ 2. Only selected students are encouraged to participate.

_____ 3. Student selection is done through standardized tests and classroom teacher recommendations.

_____ 4. An evening parent meeting is held for those desiring to have their child begin instrument instruction.

_____ 5. The evening parent meeting includes an instrument demonstration as well as a discussion of parent, teacher, and student responsibilities.

_____ 6. There is a personal interview between the teacher and parent before an instrument is rented by the parent.

_____ 7. The instrument ultimately rented is chosen only after a consultation between the parent and teacher assures it will suit the child's physical characteristics.

_____ 8. Rental payment is made before the instruments are given out.

_____ 9. A rental contract is issued stating the parent's responsibility.

_____ 10. The rental is designated for a specific period of time.

_____ 11. The rental period is carefully observed.

_____ 12. At the end of the rental period, a provision to continue in the program is made for those who cannot afford to purchase an instrument.

_____ 13. Provision number 12 is a definite policy that is carefully worked out as to who may participate.

_____ 14. If there is an infraction of the contract stipulations, procedures are established as to what actions can and will be taken.

_____ 15. Upon completion of the rental period, advice is given to parents on the purchase of instruments.

_____ 16. School instruments are replaced at regular intervals so that good conditions are maintained at all times.

_____ 17. Small repairs are handled immediately.

_____ 18. An inventory and depreciation record is kept on each instrument.

_____ 19. A provision is made to discard old instruments.

_____ 20. Sufficient instruments are available so that as many students as desire may partake of this experience.

SECTION III—THE PROGRAM

Item E—Instrument Rental Plan—from a Commercial Company

_____ 1. School authorities appoint only one company to service any one school.

_____ 2. The company chosen is decided upon after receiving written statements of company services.

_____ 3. The services are evaluated by those in charge of the school's instrumental program.

_____ 4. A written agreement is made between the school and the chosen company stating the company's and the school's responsibilities to the children and the parents to be involved in the program.

_____ 5. Only selected students are encouraged to participate.

_____ 6. Student selection is done through standardized tests and classroom teacher recommendation.

_____ 7. An evening parent meeting is held for those desiring to have their child begin instrumental study.

_____ 8. The evening parent meeting includes an instrument demonstration as well as a discussion of parent, teacher, and student responsibilities.

_____ 9. At the evening meeting, the company's educational representative discusses the company's rental-purchase plan and provides written information for parents to study.

_____ 10. The instrument a child ultimately acquires is decided upon only after a consultation between the parent, child, teacher, and the company's educational representative assures it will suit the child's physical characteristics.

_____ 11. There is a personal interview between all concerned before an instrument is rented by the parent.

_____ 12. Rental payment is made before the instrument is given to the child.

_____ 13. All monies are handled directly with the company—not through the teacher.

_____ 14. No other charges or payments are required during the trial period except the rental payment.

_____ 15. If a child has done sufficiently well to warrant his or her continuance in the instrumental program, the parent is notified by the director via a telephone call or written notice.

_____ 16. If time payments are to be made, the company provides convenient mailing envelopes.

_____ 17. Parents may return the instrument at any time, even during the bank contract period, provided all payments up to and including the date of return are made.

_____ 18. Parents are under no obligation to the company at the end of the rental period to purchase the instrument the child has been using.

_____ 19. Parents may purchase another brand, either more expensive or less expensive, if they desire.

_____ 20. Parents may purchase an instrument from another company if they so desire (the rental fee will be lost, however).

_____ 21. An insurance policy is available to cover the cost of damage or repairs during and following the rental period.

_____ 22. The company's educational representative checks the instrument being used periodically and makes minor adjustments needed without charge to the parents.

SECTION III—THE PROGRAM

Item F—Elementary Program

_____ 1. Beginning instrumental lessons are given in classes of like instruments.

_____ 2. Classes consist of not more than six students.

_____ 3. Classes are established on different levels as student advancement warrants.

_____ 4. Ambitious students are able to move up from one class level to another as proficiency increases.

_____ 5. The curriculum allows for accurate, standardized grading procedures.

_____ 6. For outstanding students, private lessons are available from qualified teachers.

_____ 7. A list of acceptable teachers outside the school system is provided by the music department to those wishing to study privately.

_____ 8. These recommended teachers are in contact with the school music department so that consistent aims and goals are assured.

_____ 9. Periodic recitals are held for students to perform solos for parents and friends.

_____ 10. Outstanding soloists participate in solo competition-festivals.

_____ 11. Outstanding soloists perform for civic and community organizations.

_____ 12. Piano teachers for the school provide accompanists for soloists.

_____ 13. The elementary school provides large ensemble experience on different levels, i.e., an "A" bands/orchestra, and a "B" band/orchestra.

_____ 14. The elementary bands/orchestras are recognized and rehearsed for performance on an elementary level, not considered as mere feeders into the junior high school.

_____ 15. The elementary organization(s) give a limited number of concerts for the school and community each year.

_____ 16. Grades are given for participation and included on the regular report card.

_____ 17. Grades for participation are based on an accurate marking procedure.

_____ 18. Grades for participation are included in overall grade averages for use in scholastic achievement awards and honors.

_____ 19. Some form of standardized test is given periodically so students, teachers, and parents can have a record of student standing.

_____ 20. Duets, trios, etc., are available for students to use as recreational playing before, during, and after school hours.

_____ 21. An all-city grade school band/orchestra augments the regular school activities, giving the more proficient students a greater challenge and wider musical experience.

_____ 22. Competition for chair positions in the advanced group is governed by definite pre-set rules, the reasons and educational objectives of which are discussed with the students.

_____ 23. Artificial stimulus is created by the use of awards for technical achievement and participation in the band/orchestra.

_____ 24. Ribbons are awarded to students when ratings at the competition-festival warrant them.

_____ 25. Participation in the instrumental program is allowed only if a child keeps up good grades in his/her other subjects.

_____ 26. Some sort of parent-teacher contact is maintained via such activities as a music section of the P.T.A., Band Mother's Club, Music Parents' Association, etc.

SECTION III—THE PROGRAM

Item G—Junior High School Program

_____ 1. Instrumental lessons are given in classes of like instruments.

_____ 2. Classes consist of not more than six students.

_____ 3. Classes are established on different levels as student advancement warrants.

_____ 4. Opportunity is made for ambitious students to move up from one class level to another as proficiency increases.

_____ 5. For outstanding students, private lessons are available from qualified teachers.

_____ 6. A list of acceptable private teachers outside the school system is provided by the music department to those who inquire.

_____ 7. These recommended teachers are in contact with the school music department so that consistent aims and goals are assured.

_____ 8. Periodic recitals are held for students to perform solos for parents and friends.

_____ 9. Outstanding soloists participate in solo competition-festivals.

_____ 10. Outstanding soloists perform for civic and community organizations.

_____ 11. Piano accompanists are provided by the piano teacher for or from the school.

_____ 12. The junior high school provides large ensemble experience on different levels, i.e., an "A" band/orchestra and "B" band/orchestra.

_____ 13. The junior high bands/orchestras are recognized and rehearsed for performances on an intermediate level, not considered as mere feeders to the high school groups.

_____ 14. The junior high organizations give a limited number of concerts for the school and community each year.

_____ 15. The junior high school band/orchestra occasionally participates in an exchange concert with junior high school groups in other school districts.

_____ 16. Grades are given for participation and included on the regular report card.

_____ 17. Grades for participation are based on an accurate marking procedure.

_____ 18. Some form of standardized test is given periodically so students, teachers, and parents can have a record of student standing.

_____ 19. Grades for participation are included in overall grade averages for use in scholastic achievement awards and honors.

_____ 20. Academic credit is given for each semester of participation in the band/orchestra.

_____ 21. Duets, trios, etc., are available for students to use as recreational playing before, during, and after school hours.

_____ 22. These ensembles are encouraged to organize on a regular basis.

_____ 23. The more proficient ensembles are allowed to participate in ensemble competition-festivals.

_____ 24. The more proficient ensembles perform for school and community organizations.

_____ 25. Challenging for chair positions in the band/orchestra is used and governed by definite, pre-set rules the reasons and educational objectives of which are discussed with the students.

_____ 26. Artificial stimulus is created by the use of awards for technical achievement, solo playing, and participation in the band/orchestra.

_____ 27. Ribbons are awarded to students when ratings at the competition-festival warrant them.

_____ 28. Participation in the instrumental program is allowed only if a child keeps up good grades in his/her other subjects.

_____ 29. Some sort of parent-teacher contact is maintained via such activities as a Band Mothers' Club, Music Parents' Association, etc.

SECTION III—THE PROGRAM

Item H—High School Program

_____ 1. The high school program consists of a five point program: full band/orchestra experience, sectional practice, technic instruction, solo playing, and chamber music (small ensemble) playing.

_____ 2. The high school band/orchestra rehearses five periods per week.

_____ 3. These periods are a minimum of forty minutes each.

_____ 4. The high school provides band/orchestra experience on different levels, i.e., an "A" band/orchestra and a "B" band/orchestra.

_____ 5. The high school organization(s) gives a minimum of four formalized concerts each year.

_____ 6. The high school band organization(s) gives a number of demonstration concerts for local elementary and junior high schools each year.

_____ 7. The high school organization(s) performs periodically for civic and community groups.

_____ 8. The high school group(s) participates in contests and festivals each year.

_____ 9. The high school band/orchestra occasionally participates in an exchange concert with bands/orchestras in other school districts.

_____ 10. Graduation credit is given for each semester of participation in the band/orchestra.

_____ 11. Grades are given for participation and included on the regular report card.

_____ 12. Grades for participation are based on an accurate marking procedure.

_____ 13. Grades for participation are included in overall grade averages used for scholastic achievement awards and honors.

_____ 14. Sectional practices are held periodically.

_____ 15. Classes in technic instruction are given to all members of the band/orchestra. (Those taking private lessons outside of school may be exempt from such lessons.)

_____ 16. These lessons are given in classes of like instruments.

_____ 17. Classes consist of not more than six students.

_____ 18. Classes are established on different levels as student advancement warrants.

_____ 19. Opportunity is made for ambitious students to move up from one class level to another as proficiency increases.

_____ 20. The program allows for accurate, standardized grading procedures.

_____ 21. For outstanding students, private lessons are available from qualified teachers.

_____ 22. A list of acceptable teachers outside the school system is provided by the music department to those who inquire.

_____ 23. These recommended teachers are in contact with the school music department so that consistent aims and goals are assured.

_____ 24. Some form of credit is given for each semester of private lessons.

_____ 25. A careful set of regulations is established for the granting of credit for private lessons.

_____ 26. A part of each lesson is devoted to playing solo material.

_____ 27. Periodic recitals are held for students to perform solos for parents and friends.

_____ 28. Outstanding soloists participate in solo competition-festivals.

_____ 29. Outstanding soloists perform for civic and community organizations.

_____ 30. The accompanists are provided by the piano teacher for or from the school.

_____ 31. Ensemble music is available for students to use as recreational playing before, during, and after school hours.

_____ 32. Ensemble playing and instruction is available to selected students in organized groups.

_____ 33. The more proficient ensembles participate in the ensemble competition-festival.

_____ 34. The more proficient ensembles perform for school assemblies and civic organizations.

_____ 35. Challenging for chair positions in the organization is used to stimulate extra practice and is governed by definite rules.

_____ 36. Artificial stimulus is created by the use of awards for technical achievement, solo playing, and participation in the organization(s).

_____ 37. Ribbons are awarded to students when ratings at the competition-festival warrant them.

_____ 38. Participation in the instrumental program is allowed only if a student keeps up good grades in his/her other subjects.

_____ 39. Some sort of parent-teacher contact is maintained via such an activity as a Band Mother's Club, Music Parents' Association, etc.

SECTION III—THE PROGRAM

Item J—Band Instrumentation

On the following tables, select only the column that is appropriate to the enrollment of the band/orchestra being evaluated. If the item called for is at the

100% level, (as that given) the evaluation would be E
75% level, (as that given) the evaluation would be S
50% level, (as that given) the evaluation would be L
25% level, (as that given) the evaluation would be V
0% level, (as that given) the evaluation would be M

The total for this area would be a composite average of all the various instruments which is entered on the work sheet under III. J. Band Instrumentation and III. K. Orchestra Instrumentation.

	School's enrollment:	200+	400+	700+
_____	1. flute	4	4	2
_____	2. oboe	1	2	2
_____	3. bassoon	1	1	2
_____	4. Eb clarinet			1
_____	5. Bb clarinet	8	8	10
_____	6. alto clarinet		2	2
_____	7. bass clarinet	1	2	2
_____	8. contrabass clarinet			1
_____	9. alto saxophone	1	2	2
_____	10. tenor saxophone	1	1	1
_____	11. baritone saxophone			1
_____	12. cornet	4	4	4
_____	13. trumpet	2	2	2
_____	14. French horn	3	4	4
_____	15. trombone	3	3	3
_____	16. bass trombone			1
_____	17. baritone	1	1	2
_____	18. tuba	2	2	2
_____	19. percussion	2	2	2
_____	20. TOTAL	35	40	50

	School's enrollment:	1000+	1500+	2000+
_____	1. flute	6	7	8
_____	2. oboe	2	2	2
_____	3. English horn	1	1	1
_____	4. bassoon	2	2	3
_____	5. contrabassoon		1	1
_____	6. Eb clarinet	1	1	1
_____	7. Bb clarinet	16	24	26
_____	8. alto clarinet	4	4	4
_____	9. bass clarinet	4	4	4
_____	10. contrabass clarinet	1	2	2
_____	11. alto saxophone	2	2	4
_____	12. tenor saxophone	1	1	1
_____	13. baritone saxophone	1	1	1

(continued)

School's enrollment:	1000+	1500+	2000+
_____ 14. cornet	4	6	6
_____ 15. trumpet	2	4	4
_____ 16. French horn	5	6	8
_____ 17. trombone	3	4	6
_____ 18. bass trombone	1	2	2
_____ 19. baritone	2	4	4
_____ 20. tuba	2	4	6
_____ 21. percussion	3	4	6
_____ 22. TOTAL	65	85	100

SECTION III—THE PROGRAM

Item K—Orchestra Instrumentation

School's enrollment:	700+	1000+	1500+	2000+
_____ 1. flute	2	2	2	2
_____ 2. flute/piccolo			1	1
_____ 3. oboe	2	2	2	2
_____ 4. oboe/English horn				1
_____ 5. Bb clarinet	2	2	2	2
_____ 6. Bb/bass clarinet				1
_____ 7. bassoon	2	2	2	2
_____ 8. French horn	2	2	4	4
_____ 9. trumpet	2	2	2	3
_____ 10. trombone	2	2	2	3
_____ 11. tuba			1	1
_____ 12. percussion	2	2	3	4
_____ 13. violion I	8	12	14	16
_____ 14. violin II	6	10	12	14
_____ 15. viola	4	6	8	10
_____ 16. cello	4	4	6	8
_____ 17. string bass	3	3	4	6
_____ 18. TOTAL	41	51	65	80

SECTION IV—SUMMER MUSIC PROGRAM

Item A—Structure

The school authorities provide a summer music program that is:

———— 1. Minimal—consisting of just private lessons.

———— 2. Partial—consisting of lessons (class and/or private) given within the confines of the school.

———— 3. Complete—consisting of lessons (class and/or private) as well as large ensemble rehearsals, i.e., band and/or orchestra.

———— 4. Maximum—a conservatory-type program of instrumental performance instruction and non-performance courses like theory, harmony, history, etc.

SECTION IV—SUMMER MUSIC PROGRAM

Item B—Location

———— 1. The program is held at a decentralized site, i.e., in the various elementary, junior and/or high schools to which students usually attend.

———— 2. The program is held at a centralized site, i.e., at one given location, most probably the high school.

———— 3. The program is held away from the usual facilities, i.e., at a summer marching band camp on a university campus or at a lake-front facility.

SECTION IV—SUMMER MUSIC PROGRAM

Item C—Financing

The summer music program is:

———— 1. Non-funded—The teacher's services are paid for directly by the students.

———— 2. The fees charged by the teacher in a non-funded program are determined by the teacher involved.

———— 3. Non-school, group funded—A tuition is charged to cover all costs of the group. For example, a marching band might raise the funds by going directly to the public and selling various items or soliciting contributions.

_____ 4. Tacitly school funded—The cash outflow is paid for by the students involved while the Board of Education provides free access to the school facilities, equipment, materials, and supplies.

_____ 5. Partial funding—A fee is paid by the participants to cover a portion of the costs while the Board of Education finances the rest.

_____ 6. Fully funded—All costs are borne by the Board of Education.

SECTION IV—SUMMER MUSIC PROGRAM

Item D—Staffing

_____ 1. Staffing is provided commensurate with the regular school year and paid for on a proportional basis i.e., proportioned to the teacher's regular yearly salary.

_____ 2. Staffing is provided to cover any extra program offerings.

_____ 3. Extra staffing is provided to cover instrumental family specialists, i.e., a woodwind specialist, a brass specialist, a percussion specialist, and/or a string specialist.

_____ 4. Extra staffing is provided to cover instrumental group specialists, i.e., a double reed specialist, a lower brass specialist, etc.

_____ 5. Extra staffing is provided to cover instrument specialists, i.e., a string bass specialist, a trombone specialist, a bassoon specialist, etc.

_____ 6. An administrative head is provided.

_____ 7. The administrative head is proportionately compensated.

SECTION IV—SUMMER MUSIC PROGRAM

Item E—Provisions for the Program

_____ 1. The school authorities have given official approval for the program.

_____ 2. School authorities have provided tacit approval for the program.

The school authorities provide use of the school. . . .

_____ 3. facilities

_____ 4. equipment

_____ 5. materials

_____ 6. supplies

The school authorities provide support personnel, i.e.,

_____ 7. janitorial services

_____ 8. bus drivers

_____ 9. grounds keepers for such things as the care and maintenance of the marching band rehearsal field

_____ 10. custodial services for setting up and tearing down things like a band shell, risers for an auditorium concert, lights for an outdoor concert, etc.

_____ 11. The teacher(s) is allowed to solicit participation in the summer program during the school day previous to the closing of school in May/June.

_____ 12. Students outside the immediate district are also allowed to participate in the program.

SECTION IV—SUMMER MUSIC PROGRAM

Item F—Course Offerings

_____ 1. Private lessons

_____ 2. Class lessons–homogeneous beginners

_____ 3. Class lessons–homogeneous elementary

_____ 4. Class lessons–homogeneous intermediate

_____ 5. Class lessons–homogeneous advanced

_____ 6. Exploratory classes for beginners

_____ 7. Exploratory classes for elementary players

_____ 8. Exploratory classes for intermediate players

_____ 9. Exploratory classes for advanced players

_____ 10. Small ensembles like flute quartets, string quartets, woodwind quintets, brass octets, etc.

_____ 11. Beginning band

_____ 12. Beginning orchestra

_____ 13. Intermediate band

_____ 14. Intermediate orchestra

_____ 15. Advanced band

_____ 16. Advanced orchestra

_____ 17. String orchestra

_____ 18. Full orchestra

_____ 19. Concert band

_____ 20. Symphony wind ensemble—a select, highly advanced group

_____ 21. Marching band

_____ 22. Rudiments of Music

_____ 23. Music theory

_____ 24. Harmony

_____ 25. Counterpoint

_____ 26. Music history

_____ 27. Music literature and appreciation

_____ 28. Performance practices

_____ 29. Solfeggio

_____ 30. Independent study

_____ 31. Recitals

_____ 32. Concerts

SECTION V—HIGH SCHOOL STAGE BAND PROGRAM

Item A—Organization

_____ 1. The stage band is reorganized each year at the conclusion of the marching band season.

_____ 2. It is reorganized only if there is qualified personnel, i.e., sufficient numbers of students with securely established embouchures and sufficient reading skills to perform this type of music.

_____ 3. The stage band rehearsals are held after school at a time convenient to those involved.

_____ 4. Only students who are regular members of the high school band are eligible to participate in the stage band with the exception of persons who play guitar, piano, or string bass.

_____ 5. Students who cease to be members of the high school concert band are also removed from the stage band.

_____ 6. Students who do not act in a responsible way toward the stage band and its purposes are summarily dismissed by the director.

_____ 7. The stage band is treated as any other small ensemble that is organized within the band program.

Stage band members are:

_____ 8. Selected by audition.

_____ 9. Those students the director has decided will benefit most from the experience and who are capable of performing in the various idioms necessary.

_____ 10. Those students who will cooperate with the director and can afford the extra time for rehearsals.

_____ 11. Those students who the director feels will be responsible members of the organization.

SECTION V—HIGH SCHOOL STAGE BAND PROGRAM

Item B—Offerings

_____ 1. Music is selected in keeping with the abilities and maturity of the members within the group.

The stage band performs music in the following idioms:

_____ 2. Big band

_____ 3. Swing, dixieland, etc.

_____ 4. Ballads, rhythm & blues

_____ 5. Peer-popular ballads, Broadway musicals

_____ 6. Classical jazz

_____ 7. Progressive jazz

_____ 8. Rock, jazz-rock, etc.

_____ 9. free-form, avant garde

_____ 10. Latin-American and its jazz counterparts

SECTION V—HIGH SCHOOL STAGE BAND PROGRAM

Item C—Instructional

_____ 1. Improvisation is taught to all the students in the group through a planned program using instructional texts specifically designed for the purpose.

_____ 2. Improvisational solos are treated to an educationally-oriented process of evaluation.

_____ 3. Skills for critical listening to various jazz idioms are developed through a planned program that uses recordings of jazz artists and groups.

SECTION V—HIGH SCHOOL STAGE BAND PROGRAM

Item D—Performances

_____ 1. The performance ratio of the stage band to other small ensembles is equally proportionate, i.e., equal performance emphasis is placed on all small ensembles, including a string quartet, brass quartet, woodwind quintet, percussion ensemble, etc.

SECTION VI—PERFORMANCES

_____ 1. Number of formal, evening concerts presented during the school year:

$$0 = M \quad 1 = V \quad 2 = L \quad 3 = S \quad 4 \text{ or more} = E$$

_____ 2. Number of school assembly-type performances presented by the band/orchestra during the school year (these may include the playing of the same materials for different schools).

M = no school concerts
V = concerts for own school
L = concerts for a few of the schools in the district
S = concerts for all the elementary schools
E = concerts for all the schools in the district including elementary, junior high and high school

_____ 3. Number of recitals held during the year for soloists and ensembles to perform for parents and friends.

$$0 = M \quad 1 = V \quad 2 = L \quad 3 = S \quad 4 \text{ or more} = E$$

_____ 4. Number of solo and ensemble performances given for school assemblies.

M = no school performances
V = for own school
L = a few performances in selected schools in the district
S = performances in all elementary schools in the district
E = performances in all the schools including elementary, junior high and high school in the district

_____ 5. The average percent of students from the band/orchestra who performed solos at the solo competition-festival.

$$0 = M \quad 1\% = V \quad 2\% = L \quad 5\% = S \quad 20\% \text{ or more} = E$$

_____ 6. The average percent of students involved in ensembles who performed for the ensemble competition-festival.

$$0 = M \quad 1\% = V \quad 4\% = L \quad 12\% = S \quad 25\% \text{ or more} = E$$

_____ 7. Percent of the students who performed as soloists for various civic and community organizations.

$$0 = M \quad 1\% = V \quad 2\% = L \quad 5\% = S \quad 10\% \text{ or more} = E$$

_____ 8. Number of ensembles performing for various civic and community organizations.

$$0 = M \quad 1\text{-}2 = V \quad 3\text{-}4 = L \quad 5\text{-}6 = S \quad 7\text{-}10 \text{ or more} = E$$

_____ 9. Number of band/orchestra members who participated in an all-county organization.

$$0 = M \quad 1 = V \quad 2 = L \quad 3 = S \quad 4 \text{ or more} = E$$

_____ 10. Number of band/orchestra members who participated in an all-state organization.

$$0 = M \quad 1 = L \quad 2 = S \quad 3 \text{ or more} = E$$

_____ 11. The average number of "classical" concerts attended by the members of the band/orchestra that were performed by a professional or semi-professional organization.

$$0 = M \quad 1 = V \quad 2 = L \quad 3 = S \quad 4 \text{ or more} = E$$

_____ 12. The average number of "classical" concerts attended by the members of the band/orchestra that were performed by a school organization.

$$0 = M \quad 1 = V \quad 2 = L \quad 3 = S \quad 4 \text{ or more} = E$$

_____ 13. The average number of "classical" recordings owned by the members of the band/orchestra.

$$0 = M \quad 1\text{-}4 = V \quad 5\text{-}6 = L \quad 7\text{-}10 = S \quad 15 \text{ or more} = E$$

SECTION VII—SCHEDULING

Item A—The Music Department Administrator

_____ 1. Plans schedules for the music staff.
_____ 2. Assists with music schedules in the local schools.
_____ 3. Works out schedule conflicts with other administrative officials.

_____ 4. Aids in insuring student participation in the rehearsals and lesson schedules.

_____ 5. Educates school personnel as to the needs and requirements necessary for carrying out an instrumental program and the necessity for rehearsal time.

SECTION VII—SCHEDULING

Item B—Pre-Band Schedule

_____ 1. Administrator establishes which classes and at what times the pre-band program is held.

_____ 2. The classes meet at least two periods per week for a sufficient amount of time to cover the average instructional book materials in one semester.

_____ 3. Class time allows the music teacher opportunity to introduce the children to the instruments to be used in the band and orchestra.

SECTION VII—SCHEDULING

Item C—Elementary School Scheduling

_____ 1. Beginning instrumental classes meet at least three periods per week.

_____ 2. Advanced beginners meet at least one period per week.

_____ 3. Each period is a minimum of forty minutes.

_____ 4. Advanced beginners are given an opportunity to participate in a formalized band/orchestra along with their class lessons.

_____ 5. The band/orchestra rehearses at least three periods per week.

_____ 6. These periods are a minimum of forty minutes each.

_____ 7. Sectional rehearsals are scheduled periodically.

_____ 8. The better wind and percussion students can participate in the orchestra.

_____ 9. If the student's ability warrants, he or she may move to a more advanced instructional class.

SECTION VII—SCHEDULING

Item D—Junior High School Schedule

_____ 1. The band/orchestra rehearses a minimum of three periods per week.

_____ 2. Technic and solo playing classes meet at least one period per week.

_____ 3. Times for small ensemble and sectional rehearsals are stipulated in the scheduling.

_____ 4. Better wind and percussion students are provided opportunities to participate in the orchestra.

_____ 5. At least two groups on different musical levels, i.e., a training band/orchestra and an advanced band/orchestra are specified in the schedule.

_____ 6. A student may move from one technic class to one more advanced if his or her ability warrants it.

_____ 7. School authorities schedule only duplicate sessions of academic classes during the band/orchestra period.

_____ 8. When static times are not available for class lessons, a rotating schedule plan is provided.

SECTION VII—SCHEDULING

Item E—High School Schedule

_____ 1. The band/orchestra rehearses five periods per week.

_____ 2. A second band/orchestra is provided for.

_____ 3. The second band/orchestra rehearses a minimum of three periods per week.

_____ 4. In addition to regular rehearsals, the schedule provides for one technic or instructional lesson per week for each member of the band/orchestra.

_____ 5. Small ensemble and sectional rehearsals are included in the schedule for each member of the band/orchestra.

_____ 6. The better wind and percussions players can rehearse with the orchestra.

_____ 7. School authorities schedule only duplicate sessions of academic classes during the band/orchestra period.

_____ 8. When static times are not available for lessons, a rotating schedule plan is used.

SECTION VIII—EQUIPMENT

Item A—Equipment Management

_____ 1. There is an established method of issuing school-owned equipment.

_____ 2. There is an established method for keeping track of school-owned equipment.

_____ 3. This system allows for instant knowledge of where each piece of equipment is being used.

_____ 4. This system makes efficient use of all equipment.

_____ 5. There is an established method of collecting all equipment.

_____ 6. There is coordinated advice given in the purchase of new equipment.

_____ 7. As school-owned instruments are purchased, every separate piece is numbered (where possible) with a permanent marking device.

_____ 8. An inventory is kept showing make, serial number, value, school number, from whom it was purchased, cost, and other pertinent information of each instrument.

_____ 9. There is a record provided for a periodic check on the condition of the instruments, the repairs made, and the names of the students to whom the instruments were issued.

SECTION VIII—EQUIPMENT

Item B—General Equipment

_____ 1. Chairs of appropriate sizes are available.

_____ 2. There are a sufficient number of music stands.

_____ 3. There is a tuning device like a stroboscope or strobotuner.

_____ 4. There is at least one metronome provided by the school.

_____ 5. Other audio-visual devices like a movie projector and film-strip projector are readily available.

_____ 6. A high quality stereophonic audio system is readily available.

_____ 7. A high quality tape recorder is readily available.

_____ 8. There is a sufficient number of mallets for all the percussion instruments.

_____ 9. There is a piano in the room where lessons are given.

SECTION VIII—EQUIPMENT

Item C—Primary Instruments

_____ 1. For the primary grades, there are sufficient instruments for rhythm band instruction, i.e., tom-toms, cymbals, triangles, castanets, etc.

_____ 2. A piano is available whenever and wherever needed.

_____ 3. Pre-band instruments are primarily purchased by the individual students in the classes.

_____ 4. A few pre-band instruments are purchased by the school for those students who may not be able to secure their own.

SECTION VIII—EQUIPMENT

Item D—Elementary Instruments

The elementary school provides. . . .

_____ 1. sufficient numbers of flutes

_____ 2. at least four oboes

_____ 3. sufficient numbers of clarinets

_____ 4. at least two alto clarinets

_____ 5. at least two bass clarinets

_____ 6. at least two bassoons

_____ 7. sufficient numbers of alto saxophones

_____ 8. at least one tenor saxophone

_____ 9. sufficient numbers of cornets

_____ 10. sufficient numbers of French horns

_____ 11. sufficient numbers of trombones

_____ 12. sufficient numbers of baritones

_____ 13. sufficient numbers of tubas

_____ 14. sufficient numbers of half-size violins

_____ 15. sufficient numbers of three-quarter size violins

_____ 16. sufficient numbers of full-size violins

_____ 17. sufficient numbers of small violas

_____ 18. sufficient numbers of medium-size violas

_____ 19. sufficient numbers of full-size violas

_____ 20. sufficient numbers of half-size cellos

_____ 21. sufficient numbers of three-quarter size cellos

_____ 22. sufficient numbers of full-size cellos

_____ 23. sufficient numbers of half-size string basses

_____ 24. sufficient numbers of three-quarter size string basses

_____ 25. two snare drums

_____ 26. one bass drum

_____ 27. one set of crash cymbals

_____ 28. one suspended cymbal and stand

_____ 29. a sufficient number of mallets for all the percussion instruments

_____ 30. one set of timpani

_____ 31. a sufficient number of traps, e.g., wood blocks, tambourines, triangles, etc.

_____ 32. a sufficient number of Latin-American percussion instruments, e.g., maracas, claves, bongo drums, etc.

_____ 33. at least one mallet percussion instrument such as a xylophone or marimba.

_____ 34. a set of orchestra bells.

SECTION VIII—EQUIPMENT

Item E—Junior High School Instruments

The school provides at least. . . .

_____ 1. one piccolo

_____ 2. four oboes

_____ 3. two bassoons

_____ 4. two alto clarinets

_____ 5. two bass clarinets

_____ 6. four French horns

_____ 7. four baritones

_____ 8. four tubas

_____ 9. four violas

_____ 10. four cellos

_____ 11. four string basses

_____ 12. one bass drum

_____ 13. two snare drums

_____ 14. one set of crash cymbals

_____ 15. one suspended cymbal

_____ 16. a sufficient number of mallets for all the percussion instruments

_____ 17. one set of timpani

_____ 18. a sufficient number of traps, e.g., wood blocks, tambourines, triangles, etc.

_____ 19. a sufficient number of Latin-American percussion instruments, e.g., maracas, claves, bongo drums, etc.

_____ 20. at least one mallet percussion instrument such as a xylophone or marimba

_____ 21. a set of orchestra bells

_____ 22. a piano

SECTION VIII—EQUIPMENT

Item F—High School Instruments

The school provides at least. . . .

_____ 1. two piccolos

_____ 2. four oboes

_____ 3. one English horn

_____ 4. four bassoons

_____ 5. one contrabassoon

_____ 6. one Eb soprano clarinet

_____ 7. sufficient numbers of alto clarinets

_____ 8. sufficient numbers of bass clarinets

_____ 9. two contrabass clarinets

_____ 10. one soprano saxophone

_____ 11. one tenor saxophone

_____ 12. one baritone saxophone

_____ 13. two single French horns

_____ 14. four double French horns

_____ 15. four baritones

_____ 16. sufficient numbers of tubas

_____ 17. sufficient numbers of violas

_____ 18. sufficient numbers of cellos

_____ 19. sufficient numbers of string basses

_____ 20. one bass drum

_____ 21. one bass drum stand

_____ 22. one shallow snare drum

_____ 23. one deep snare drum

_____ 24. one pair of large concert crash cymbals

_____ 25. one pair of medium concert crash cymbals

_____ 26. one pair finger cymbals

_____ 27. one large suspended cymbal

_____ 28. one medium suspended cymbal

_____ 29. one symphonic gong

_____ 30. one 32-inch timpani

_____ 31. one 29-inch timpani

_____ 32. one 26-inch timpani

_____ 33. one 23-inch timpani

_____ 34. one 8-inch triangle

_____ 35. one 6-inch triangle

_____ 36. three sets of triangle beaters

_____ 37. one set of chimes

_____ 38. one xylophone

_____ 39. one marimba

_____ 40. one celesta

_____ 41. one set, 4 pitches tom-toms

_____ 42. a large selection of Latin-American traps including maracas, bongo-drums, claves, etc.

SECTION VIII—EQUIPMENT

Item G—Marching Band Instruments

The school provides sufficient numbers of. . . .

_____ 1. alto horns to replace the French horns used for concert band

_____ 2. metal or composition-type clarinets for students who own wooden instruments

_____ 3. alto and tenor saxophones for students who play oboe, bassoon, or lower clarinets

_____ 4. sousaphones

_____ 5. field drums

_____ 6. tenor drums

_____ 7. marching bass drums

_____ 8. marching band cymbals

_____ 9. specialty drums

SECTION VIII—EQUIPMENT

Item H—Conditions of Instruments

Whenever evaluating the instruments, use the following formulas: If the instruments average ten or more years old, the instruments are to be scored as M. If they are from seven to nine years old, the score is to be V, even if their condition is good (because of repeated repairs and overhauling). If the instruments are under seven years old, score as follows: E = excellent condition, S = good condition, L = fair condition, M = poor condition.

_____ 1. flutes

_____ 2. flute cases

_____ 3. oboes

_____ 4. oboe cases

_____ 5. clarinets

_____ 6. clarinet mouthpieces

_____ 7. clarinet cases

_____ 8. saxophones

_____ 9. saxophone mouthpieces

_____ 10. saxophone cases

_____ 11. bassoons

_____ 12. bassoon bocals

_____ 13. bassoon cases

_____ 14. cornets

_____ 15. cornet mouthpieces

_____ 16. cornet cases

_____ 17. French horns

_____ 18. French horn mouthpieces

_____ 19. French horn cases

_____ 20. trombones

_____ 21. trombone mouthpieces

_____ 22. trombone cases

_____ 23. baritones

_____ 24. baritone mouthpieces

_____ 25. baritone cases

_____ 26. tubas

_____ 27. tuba mouthpieces

_____ 28. tuba cases

_____ 29. snare drums

_____ 30. snare drum stands

_____ 31. snare drum cases

_____ 32. bass drum

_____ 33. bass drum stand

_____ 34. bass drum storage cover

_____ 35. bass drum beaters

_____ 36. timpani

_____ 37. timpani storage covers

_____ 38. timpani mallets

_____ 39. cymbals

_____ 40. percussion traps

_____ 41. trap storage facility

_____ 42. violins

_____ 43. violin bows

_____ 44. violin cases

_____ 45. violas

_____ 46. viola bows

_____ 47. viola cases

_____ 48. cellos

_____ 49. cello bows

_____ 50. cellos cases

_____ 51. string basses

_____ 52. string bass bows

_____ 53. string bass cases

SECTION VIII—EQUIPMENT

Item J—Marching Band Equipment

_____ 1. A voice gun, bull horn, portable amplifier, or other electronic device is available to aid the director while giving directions on the rehearsal field.

_____ 2. There is a set of yard-line markers for the marching band rehearsal field.

_____ 3. There is a plotting board for use in setting up marching band shows.

_____ 4. There is a stop watch for timing shows.

_____ 5. A portable microphone is available so announcements for the band may be made from the field during the half-time show.

_____ 6. A facsimile machine of some kind is available for making show charts for the band members.

_____ 7. There is sufficient equipment to make up professional looking marching band charts.

_____ 8. Movie-making and viewing equipment is available for studying the marching band performance.

_____ 9. There is a sufficient number of marching band folders.

_____ 10. There are special racks for sorting and storing the marching band music and folders.

_____ 11. There is a portable field podium.

_____ 12. There is a field tower for viewing the band during rehearsals.

_____ 13. There are tools and equipment for making props.

_____ 14. There is sufficient color guard equipment, e.g., guns, flags, flag straps, and uniforms.

_____ 15. There is a sufficient number of uniforms so that each marching band member is assured of a good fit.

SECTION IX—MATERIALS AND SUPPLIES

_____ 1. Instruction books for lessons are purchased by the students.

_____ 2. All music used by major organizations and small ensembles is purchased by the school.

_____ 3. There are sufficient numbers of recording tapes for instructional purposes that retain examples for future reference.

_____ 4. There is a library of recordings for use in the instructional program.

_____ 5. There is a film library for instructional purposes.

_____ 6. Sufficient amounts of duplication materials are available.

_____ 7. There are sufficient amounts of paper for duplicating materials.

_____ 8. Specialized duplication materials, like those with staff lines, are available.

_____ 9. Such classroom items as chalk, staff-line markers, etc., are provided.

_____ 10. A chalkboard with and without staff lines is available.

_____ 11. Manuscript paper is provided in sufficient quantity for use in the instructional program.

_____ 12. Sufficient supplies, materials, and funds are available for printing and/or duplicating concert programs.

_____ 13. Sufficient materials are available for storage to keep music in order and readily available.

_____ 14. Music folders are provided and replaced regularly to keep music as soil-free as possible.

_____ 15. Sufficient materials and supplies are available for keeping in contact with parents of students involved in the program.

SECTION X—FACILITIES

Item A—Concert Band/Orchestra

The rehearsal room . . .

_____ 1. is a designated space not used by other classes or activities

_____ 2. is designated specifically for instrumental music rehearsals

_____ 3. is undisturbed by other areas of instruction and activities during the school year

_____ 4. is located in an area segregated acoustically from academic classes

_____ 5. is accessible to the auditorium

_____ 6. has direct entry/exit to outside

_____ 7. contains lavatory and drinking facilities

_____ 8. has all music areas in proximity

_____ 9. is at least 1500 square feet in size

_____ 10. allows 20 square feet per student and a minimum of 260 cubic feet per student

_____ 11. is at least 30 feet in depth

_____ 12. ceiling is at least 14 feet, but does not exceed 18 feet

_____ 13. contains risers with a width of five feet

_____ 14. contains risers with safety strapping along the front edge

_____ 15. temperature is thermostatically controlled at a constant 68°-70°F

_____ 16. heating vents are fire-proofed

_____ 17. heating vents are not connected to other classrooms

_____ 18. heating vents are acoustically treated

——— 19. has easy access to fresh air

——— 20. air conditioning provides humidity of 40–60%

——— 21. air conditioning controls are in the music area

——— 22. has natural lighting from east or west

——— 23. has artificial light that is indirect or fluorescent with a minimum of 50 foot candles

——— 24. has its acoustics controlled by special wall materials, tiles, and/or draperies

The practice rooms . . .

——— 25. number a minimum of three

——— 26. contain pianos

——— 27. are a minimum of 8 feet by 10 feet

——— 28. have soundproof doors, walls, floors, ceilings, and windows

——— 29. have good ventilation and adequate lighting

A band/orchestra office . . .

——— 30. is provided

——— 31. size is a minimum of 10 feet by 10 feet

——— 32. contains a desk, chairs, filing and storage equipment, secretarial desk, and telephone

——— 33. has a window to the rehearsal area

——— 34. has communication to all parts of the school

Ancillary rooms include . . .

——— 35. an instrument room or facility

——— 36. a repair facility containing a work bench, cabinets, instrument storage, tools, gas, water, and electric connections

SECTION X—FACILITIES

Item B—Marching Band Facilities

——— 1. A rehearsal field is in close proximity to the regular rehearsal room.

——— 2. The field is rather secluded so as not to disturb academic classes.

——— 3. There is a storage facility next to the rehearsal field for drums, sousaphones, props, etc.

_____ 4. The field is graded regularly, kept in good condition, and covered with a good quality of sturdy grass.

_____ 5. The field is lined regularly by the grounds keeper(s).

_____ 6. There is working space for making props.

_____ 7. There is storage space for props.

_____ 8. Space in the football stands is marked off and properly policed so the band is assured sufficient room during the course of the football game.

SECTION X—FACILITIES

Item C—Storage Facilities

If a separate instrument storage room is available. . . .

_____ 1. it is a minimum of 20 feet by 30 feet with windows on one side.

_____ 2. lockers (with locks) are placed along both walls of the room with numbers and sizes determined by the types of instruments to be stored.

_____ 3. lockers extend to the ceiling for storage of seldom-used equipment.

_____ 4. all lockers are covered with felt or rubber at the bottom.

_____ 5. room temperature is kept at 68-70°F, with relative humidity of 40-50%.

_____ 6. the room should open into the rehearsal room via double oversized doors.

_____ 7. special racks are available for large instruments like sousaphones, tubas, etc.

If a separate storage room is not available. . . .

_____ 8. lockers of various sizes are built in the rehearsal room near the instruments they serve.

_____ 9. the lockers are built only around the side and back walls of the rehearsal room.

_____ 10. cabinets, free from any obstruction at floor level, are provided for the timpani, marimba, xylophone, etc.

_____ 11. these cabinets are large enough so that instruments can be rolled easily into them.

_____ 12. the music library, located near the director's office.

_____ 13. the music library at a minimum size of 20 feet by 30 feet.

_____ 14. equipment in the library such as a work table, sorting racks, music and supply cabinets, chairs, a paper cutter, a typewriter, mending tape dispenser, etc.

_____ 15. file cabinets available in legal and letter sizes

_____ 16. closed cabinets built above file cabinets for additional storage.

_____ 17. mobile sorting racks with slanting shelves.

_____ 18. a special cabinet for percussion equipment.

The percussion cabinet . . .

_____ 19. has rubber casters and shelves of various sizes

_____ 20. has a special shelf for orchestra bells

_____ 21. has a special shelf for cymbals

_____ 22. has doors with secure locks

_____ 23. has side handles for ease in transportation

_____ 24. has a padded top

_____ 25. All percussion equipment and instruments that are not stored in the cabinet have covers and/or cases for storage purposes.

_____ 26. The uniforms are stored in a separate room with easy access.

_____ 27. The uniform racks allow for a four-inch space between each uniform.

_____ 28. The racks allow for the coat and trousers to be hung separately.

_____ 29. The racks allow for sufficient space to store hats, plumes, and miscellaneous items.

_____ 30. The uniform room is moth and dust proof.

_____ 31. There is sufficient ventilation in the uniform room.

_____ 32. There is a dutch door entry to the uniform room.

SECTION XI—INSTRUMENTAL BUDGET

Item A—Staffing

● A rating of E is given if staffing exceeds the guidelines, i.e., the teacher(s) has student contact that averages to be less than 125 student contacts per week. This shows staffing is more than adequately provided for under the budget allocations.

● A rating of S is given if staffing meets the guidelines, i.e., the teacher(s) has student contact that averages to be five periods per day with a total of 125 to 150 student contacts per week. This shows that, for the most part, proper staffing is provided.

● A rating of *L* is given if the staffing does not meet the guidelines and is such that the teacher(s) has student contact that averages to be more than five periods per day or averages between 150 to 200 students. Staffing in this case is considered to be limited.

● A rating of *V* is given if the staffing results in a teacher(s) having student contact of more than six periods per day with an average of over 200 student contacts per week. Under these conditions, staffing is considered in need of expansion.

● A rating of *M* is given if the staffing exceeds the six period day and the teacher(s) average about 250 student contacts per week. Staffing in this case is considered in very poor condition.

SECTION XI—INSTRUMENTAL BUDGET

Item B—Administration of Budget

_____ 1. All funds are handled by persons other than the director(s) of the major ensembles or the instrumental instructor(s).

_____ 2. Requisitions for equipment, music, supplies, materials, and services are made with a limited amount of time consumption.

_____ 3. Emergency equipment may be purchased without prior approval.

_____ 4. A petty cash fund is at hand for miscellaneous items.

SECTION XI—INSTRUMENTAL BUDGET

Item C—Equipment

_____ 1. Funds to purchase instruments are sufficient for the functioning of the department.

_____ 2. Funds to purchase accessories are sufficient for the functioning of the department.

_____ 3. Funds for instrument repair and overhaul are sufficient for the functioning of the department.

_____ 4. A uniform layaway fund allows for periodic replacement of uniforms.

_____ 5. Bids are taken when supplies and equipment purchases exceed $100.00.

_____ 6. Emergency equipment may be purchased without prior approval.

SECTION XI—INSTRUMENTAL BUDGET

Item D—Materials and Supplies

——— 1. Funds for the purchase of new music are sufficient for the size and enrollment of the department.

——— 2. Funds for office supplies are sufficient.

——— 3. Funds for the purchase of teaching supplies are sufficient.

——— 4. Sufficient funds are available for the purchase of awards.

SECTION XI—INSTRUMENTAL BUDGET

Item E—Activities and Fees

——— 1. Transportation funds are sufficient for the functioning of the department.

——— 2. Allocations of funds for insurance are sufficient for the needs of the department.

——— 3. Sufficient funds are available for entrance fees.

——— 4. Extra funds are placed at the disposal of the organization(s) for participating in athletic events, festivals, and exchange concerts.

SECTION XI—INSTRUMENTAL BUDGET

Item F—Distribution of Funds

——— 1. Funds are distributed proportionately between the band and orchestra programs in regard to student enrollments and frequency of public appearances.

——— 2. 27.5% of the budget is allocated for instrument purchases.

——— 3. 15% of the budget is allocated for music.

——— 4. 4% of the budget is allocated for accessories.

——— 5. 10% of the budget is allocated for instrument repair and overhaul.

——— 6. 9.5% of the budget is allocated for transportation.

——— 7. 15% of the budget is allocated for uniform layaway.

——— 8. 3% of the budget is allocated for insurance.

——— 9. 3% of the budget is allocated for special fees, i.e., contests, festivals, etc.

——— 10. 4% of the budget is allocated for awards.

——— 11. 1% of the budget is allocated for office supplies.

——— 12. 8% of the budget is allocated for miscellaneous items.

CRITERION MODEL #2

METHOD BOOK EVALUATION

The following charts allow for up to eight method books to be compared at one time.

After deciding which methods will be compared, each will be assigned a code number to correspond with the numbers at the top of each evaluative column.

To evaluate 'Introductory Materials' (Section A), and 'Technical and Melodic Materials' (Section B), the following letters would be used:

> E — Extensive treatment
> S — Some treatment
> L — Limited treatment
> M — Missing and needed
> N — Not necessary or desirable

For 'Introduction of Notes and Rhythms' (Section C) and 'Miscellaneous Fundamentals' (Section D), the actual page and line number will be entered. In order to solve the problem caused by inconsistent numbering of exercises, each line of music in each book being analyzed should be numbered.

For the items in Section E, use A for 'excellent,' B for 'very good,' C for 'good,' D for 'fair' and F for 'poor.'

The final determination as to which method is best cannot be made in clearly established numerical outcomes. The determination as to which method is used can only be made by scrutinizing all the ratings and determining which seems to fit most closely that which is desired. The determination will come not from a numerical outcome but from the knowledge of each book that is gained through studying the information contained in each and comparing its attributes with the items listed in the charts.*

*© 1971 by The Instrumentalist Co. Reprinted by permission from *The Instrumentalist*, August, 1971. Subscriptions are available from The Instrumentalist Co., 200 Northfield Road, Northfield, Illinois, USA.

SECTION A—INTRODUCTORY MATERIALS

	Methods (code numbers)							
	1	2	3	4	5	6	7	8
Theory								
Terminology								
Rhythm								
Suggestions to players								
Care of the instrument								
Fingering chart								
Explanation of fingering chart								
Illustrations								
embouchure								
picture of the instrument								
playing position								
hand position								
Other fundamentals								
Teacher's manual								
Conductor's part								
Piano accompaniment book								

SECTION B—TECHNICAL AND MELODIC MATERIALS

	Methods (code numbers)							
	1	2	3	4	5	6	7	8
Introduction of new notes								
Practice of new tones								
Exercises (drills)								
use of scales								
use of arpeggios								
use of chromatic								
mechanism studies								
lip slurs								
Review materials								
Supplementary materials								
Solo materials								
Piano accompaniment in the parts								
Ensemble materials								
Use of known tunes								
Use of newly composed tunes								
Use of testing materials								
Clearly defined assignments								

SECTION C—INTRODUCTION OF NOTES AND RHYTHMS

	Methods (code numbers)							
	1	2	3	4	5	6	7	8
Starting tone								
2nd tone introduced								
3rd tone introduced								
4th tone introduced								
5th tone introduced								
Range of the entire book								
first quarter								
first half								
Introduction of rhythmic figures								
whole note								
whole rest								
half note								
half rest								
dotted half note								
quarter note								
quarter rest								
dotted quarter note								
eighth notes								
sixteenth notes								
dotted eighth and sixteenth notes								

SECTION D—MISCELLANEOUS FUNDAMENTALS

	\multicolumn{8}{c}{Methods (code numbers)}
	1	2	3	4	5	6	7	8
First appearance of key signatures								
First accidentals								
Meter signatures:								
4/4								
2/4								
3/4								
6/8, 9/8, or 12/8								
6/8 in two								
Dynamics								
accents								
crescendo								
diminuendo								
piano								
forte								
mezzo forte/piano								
Articulation								
ties								
slurs								
staccato								
Tempo markings like allegro, largo, etc.								
Repeat signs								
First and second endings								
Fermata								

SECTION E—APPEARANCE OF THE BOOK

	1	2	3	4	5	6	7	8
General appearance is attractive								
Illustrations are attractive								
Illustrations are done in good taste								
Illustrations are accurately done								
Printing is clear and clean								
Pages are uncluttered								
There is sufficient space between lines								
Staff and notes are large enough for easy reading								

Methods (code numbers)

CRITERION MODEL #3

Checklist for
JUDGING QUALITY MUSIC*

This checklist makes it possible to compare the quality of several compositions though no "final grade" can be given as to how "high" the quality of a composition might be.

Step 1: Write the names of the compositions to be evaluated on the top line of several check sheets like that provided.

Step 2: Evaluate the compositions as either "having" or "not having" the particular attributes listed. If a composition has, for example, the attribute listed as number one, "subtleties in the musical ideas and in their treatment. . . .", put a check mark in the left-hand box. If the composition does not have this attribute, place a zero in the right-hand box.

Step 3: After the compositions have been evaluated, add up the number of checkmarks and zeros and enter them in the big boxes at the bottom of the second page.

No final outcome can be arrived at. However, through this method, various compositions can be evaluated as to their comparative worth. The compositions having the most checkmarks would thus appear to be musically more valuable than those having fewer checkmarks.

*© 1965 by The Instrumentalist Co. Reprinted by permission from *The Instrumentalist*, December 1965. Subscriptions are available from The Instrumentalist Co., 200 Northfield Road, Northfield, Illinois, USA.

Checklist for
JUDGING QUALITY MUSIC

NAME OF THE COMPOSITION

Has	Does not have	
☐	☐	1. subtleties in the musical ideas and in their treatment : is not straight-forward and easily anticipated
☐	☐	2. a quality of durability : lasting value : one can grow into it rather than out of it : not likely to be discarded
☐	☐	3. elements of imagination : through it one constantly finds new beauty : it stretches the imagination and creative powers : its depth is not fully realized easily and quickly
☐	☐	4. the compositional devices of unity versus variety
☐	☐	5. an idiom without overworked cliches : melodic, harmonic, or rhythmic : freshness and value
☐	☐	6. an avoidance of meaningless repetition of trite phrases
☐	☐	7. thematic material with possibilities for development and manipulation
☐	☐	8. a melodic line with interesting rise and fall, effective intervals, and balance
☐	☐	9. a balance between tension and relaxation revealed in the harmonic movement : excites feelings in the listeners
☐	☐	10. harmonies that are complex enough to challenge the musical thought of the individual
☐	☐	11. rhythms with vitality and variety
☐	☐	12. rhythms with some complexities
☐	☐	13. some complexity of form with subtle relationships among the different parts
☐	☐	14. is in good taste for the particular occasion
☐	☐	15. follows the greatest opportunity for the artistic expression of its musical ideas
☐	☐	16. a concept that is large and challenging : the simplicity of a song by Schubert for example, is large in concept and challenges the performer to express its deep understanding
☐	☐	17. different parts that are from the same origins, shaped by the same thought : style evolves when there is organized cohesion among its different parts
☐	☐	18. melody, harmony, rhythm, and form that is integrated into a expressive whole in which no one element predominates, but all play their logical role in an aesthetic expression

RESULTS

Number of "Has" _____   Number of "Does Not Have" _____

CRITERION MODEL #4

DEFINING THE *DoD* OF BAND COMPOSITIONS

The following provides criteria for defining the *DoD* (Degree *of* Technical and Musical *D*ifficulty) of a band composition. The spectrum of difficulty of band compositions is divided into six degrees. These degrees approximate the following verbal descriptions:

> *DoD*–1 = very easy
> *DoD*–2 = easy
> *DoD*–3 = medium easy
> *DoD*–4 = moderately difficult
> *DoD*–5 = difficult
> *DoD*–6 = very difficult

There are seven categories used to determine the *DoD* of a musical composition. They include:

> A—Key Signature
> B—Meter Signature
> C—Tempo
> D—Rhythm Patterns
> E—Instrument Range
> F—Fatigue Factor
> G—Instrumentation

There are four components that make up the Fatigue Factor. They include:

> 1. Performance Time
> 2. Metronomic Counts
> 3. Note-Head Count
> 4. Musical Condiments

The procedure for establishing the *DoD* of a composition is to secure a series of P-DoD-V (Partial *DoD* Values) for each of the items as follows:*

1. Prepare the necessary work sheets as given here and enter the name of the composition to be evaluated on each sheet. The work sheets needed will include:

*(1) through (24) are based on the research of Duane E. Wareham for D.Ed. dissertation at Pennsylvania State University, 1967, THE DEVELOPMENT AND EVALUATION OF OBJECTIVE CRITERIA FOR GRADING BAND MUSIC INTO SIX LEVELS OF DIFFICULTY, Ann Arbor, Michigan, University Microfilms, Inc., 1982.

DoD Work Sheet. . . .

#1—Categories A through D

#2—Category E

#3—Category F (Performance Time)

#4—Category F (Metronomic Counts)

#5—Category F (Note-Head/Condiment Count)

#6—Category F (Composite Note-Head/Condiment Count)

#7—Category F

#8—Final Outcome

2. On each of the two *DoD* Work Sheets #5 and #6, check one for each of the items it will be used for—one for the note-head count, and one for the condiment count.

3. Complete *DoD* Work Sheet #1 for the key signature, meter signature, tempo, rhythm patterns, and instrument range.

4. Enter all the concert key signatures that appear in the composition in the space provided for *DoD* Category A. If it is a multi-movement composition, include the key signature of all the movements.

5. Compare the keys of the composition with the ingredients found on page 124.

6. Enter that finding—the *P-DoD-V* (Partial *DoD* Value)—on the appropriate line on *DoD* Work Sheet #8—Final Outcomes.

FOR CATEGORY B—METER SIGNATURE

7. Enter the meter signatures that appear in the composition in the space provided for *DoD* Category B.

8. Compare the keys of the composition with the ingredients found on page 124.

9. Enter that finding (the *P-DoD-V*) on the appropriate line on *DoD* Work Sheet #8—Final Outcomes.

FOR CATEGORY C—ITALIANESQUE TEMPO INDICATORS

10. Enter the Italianesque tempo indicators that appear in the complete composition (all movements) in the space provided for *DoD* Category C. Do not include such things as ritardando, rallentando, accelerando, etc.

11. Compare the Italianesque tempo indicators found in the composition with the ingredients found on page 124.

12. Enter that finding (the *P-DoD-V*) on the appropriate line on *DoD* Work Sheet #8—Final Outcomes.

FOR CATEGORY D—RHYTHM PATTERNS

13. Enter significant rhythm patterns found in the composition in the space provided for *DoD* Category D.

14. Compare the rhythm patterns found in the composition with the ingredients found on page 125 to 129.

15. Enter that finding (the *P-DoD-V*) on the appropriate line on *DoD* Work Sheet #8—Final Outcomes.

FOR CATEGORY E—INSTRUMENT RANGE

16. On *DoD* Work Sheet #2, enter the highest and lowest notes that appear in each of the instrument parts indicated.

For purposes of this survey, staffless notation is used. The style used is that whereby middle C is designated as C/5. A complete description of this is given on page 130.

17. Compare the range of each instrument found in the composition with the ingredients found on page 131.

18. Enter those findings (the *P-DoD-V*) on the appropriate lines on the Instrument Range Work Sheets after each instrument.

19. Secure an average *P-DoD-V* for all the instruments by using the formula at the bottom of *DoD* Work Sheet #2.

20. Enter that single *P-DoD-V* figure on the appropriate line on *DoD* Work Sheet #8—Final Outcomes.

FOR CATEGORY F—FATIGUE FACTOR

The fatigue factor is made up of three components. (1) Performance Time, (2) Metronomic Counts, (3) Note-Head Count, and (4) Condiment Count. Step #21 through #28 need not be completed if the composer or editor has indicated the duration of the composition on the score. If the duration is given, convert that time into seconds—which would become the Numerical Time Factor. For example, if the performance time is given as 3½ minutes, the Numerical Time Factor would be $60 \times 3 + 30 = 210$, i.e., 60 seconds in a minute—times three minutes—plus the 30 seconds more in a half minute equals 210. Enter that number on *DoD* Work Sheet #7 − FF #1 − Performance Time.

FOR FATIGUE FACTOR COMPONENT #1— PERFORMANCE TIME

21. Label the beginning of each major and minor sectional change with an upper case letter. Any change of tempo or meter constitutes a sectional change for purposes of determining the Performance Time. If the composition is a multi-

movement work, start the second movement lettering in continuous sequence with the first movement's last sub-section. For example, if the first movement has two tempo changes and a meter change, that would constitute four sub-sections. Thus the second movement would be the start of section *E*—for the purposes herein. When using alphaletters for this purpose, do not use the letter "I" or the letter "O" as these can be confused with the number "one" and the number zero. Thus the letters to be used would be: A, B, C, D, E, F, G, H, J, K, L, M, N, P, Q, etc.

22. Count the number of measures in each section and enter that finding in the appropriate boxes on the *DoD* Work Sheet #3 (FF #1—Fatigue Factor #1).

23. Enter the meter-count of each section in the appropriate boxes on *DoD* Work Sheet #3 (FF #2).

24. Multiply the number of measures in each section (FF #1) by the meter-count in each section (FF #2) and enter the totals in the appropriate boxes under FF #3—the Gross Meter-Count. Multiply FF #1, Sec. *A* FF #2, Sec. *A* to arrive at FF #3, Sec. *A*. Likewise, FF #1, Sec. *B* would be multiplied by FF #2, Sec. *B* to arrive at FF #3, Sec. *B*.

25. Establish a metronome setting for each numbered section (if not provided) and enter that numerical tempo in the appropriate boxes under FF #4.

Following are some guidelines for converting Italianesque tempo indicators into metronome number.

> Largo. . . . . .40—60
> Largetto . . . . .60—66
> Adagio . . . . .66—76
> Andante . . . . .76—108
> Moderato . . . . .108—120
> Allegro . . . . .120—168
> Presto . . . . .168—200
> Prestissimo . . . . .200—208

Because there is a wide range of metronome settings possible in each Italianesque tempo indicator, it may be necessary to establish an "average" tempo. For example, if a section of a composition is labeled Andante, do this: Arrive at a metronome setting for a "fast" Andante (for the section in question) then a "slow" Andante. Use the average of the "fast" Andante and "slow" Andante for FF #4.

When taking steps to establish the composite tempo, it is not necessary to try to account for temporal changes due to such things as a ritardando, accelerando, fermata, et al.

26. Divide the gross meter-count (FF #3) in each section by the metronomic settings (FF #4) in each section and enter those findings in the appropriate sectional boxes on *DoD* Work Sheet #8—FF #5 (Sectional Time Factors).

27. Following the formula at the bottom of *DoD* Work Sheet #3, add all the

individual sectional time factors (FF #5) together. Multiply that figure by sixty. This equals the Numerical Time Factor (FFC #1).

28. Enter that finding (the *P-DoD-V*) on the appropriate line on *DoD* Work Sheet #7.

FOR FATIGUE FACTOR COMPONENT #2— METRONOMIC COUNT

29. Establish the metronomic count with the use of *Dod* Work Sheet #4. If the composition has numerous meter changes that result in different numbers of beats per measure, code each of those changes by writing "MC-2" (for Meter Change-1), MC-3, MC-4, etc. on the score at each point of change. (MC-1 would be entered at the beginning of the composition—i.e., the first measure.)

30. Using *DoD* Work Sheet #4, enter the meter count in the first of the three connected boxes.

31. Count the number of measures in each of those coded sections and enter that number in the center of the appropriate three connected boxes.

32. Multiply the meter count (1st box) by the number of measures (center box) and enter that number in the 3rd box. This becomes the "Sectional Metronomic Count." (See Illustration 1.)

33. Add all the sectional metronomic counts together and enter that total at the bottom of the Work Sheet (FFC #2).

34. Enter that total on the appropriate line on *DoD* Work Sheet 7–Composite Fatigue Factor.

FOR FATIGUE FACTOR COMPONENT #3— NOTE-HEAD COUNT

35. Establish the note-head count with the use of *DoD* Work Sheets #5. Only a sample number (every fifth measure) will be used for establishing the note-head count.

36. With the First Flute part in hand, number every fifth measure, i.e., label measure 1, measure 5, measure 10, measure 15, measure 20, etc. A full score could be used instead of individual parts, thus saving the need for numbering seven individual parts. If it is a multi-movement work, the measures of succeeding movements are to be numbered consecutively with the first. For example, if the first movement ends with measure 128, the first measure of the second movement is to be measure number 129. If there is a D.C. or D.S., number the "repeated" measures as consecutive, i.e., as though they were written out.

It is possible that the survey measures during a D.C. or D.S. will be different from the survey measures so labeled the first time over the same material. Thus on a D.C. or D.S., the note head-count could be taken in different survey measures.

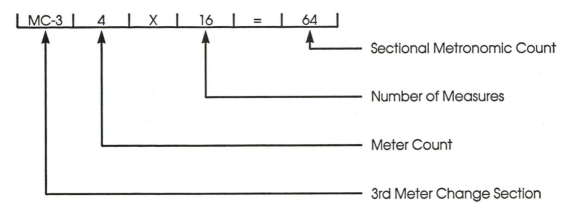

Illustration 1

37. Count the number of note heads in each survey measure. Enter the findings in the appropriate boxes on *DoD* Work Sheet #5. For example, if there is a rhythmic figure in 6/8 that appears like this:

the note head-count would be "six". If a measure in 4/4 had a rhythmic figure like this:

the note head-count would be "nine." Notes connected by ties are to be counted separately. For example, this measure: 3/4

would have a note head-count of "three." If a quarter note is tied to an eighth note, that would count for two notes even though the figure really makes for one tone. For the snare drum, count the strokes played regardless of whether it is a roll or a flam. If a five-stroke roll consists of a quarter note tied to an eighth, that would count for five note-heads. If the eighth note appeared in the next measure, i.e., the 5th stroke of the five-stroke roll appeared in the next measure, the note head count would only be four. A flam consists of a "grace" note connected to a quarter note, thus two note-heads would be counted. If the survey measure contains a full measure of rest, a zero is to be entered in the appropriate measure number (m.#"). If there were to appear a single eighth-note in a survey measure of 12/8 with eleven counts of rest, the note head-count for that measure would be "one." If there are repeated sections, do not count them for this factor—use only repeated measures that are part of a D.C. or D.S.

If a survey measure falls on a first and second ending, use the second ending for survey purposes.

38. Add the findings for the surveyed measures of each instrument together and enter the grand total on the appropriate line on *DoD* Work Sheet #6.

39. Using *DoD* Work Sheet #6, secure the composite note-head count.

40. Enter the note-head count for each instrument on *DoD* Work-Sheet #6 on the appropriate lines.

41. Add the counts for each individual instrument together and divide by seven (as indicated). This provides the composite (average) note-head count.

If there was no note-head count for the snare drum, divide the total of the six other instruments by six. If there is no significant drum part, that component may be dropped. If the timpani is used exclusively or to a much greater extent than the snare drum, the note-head count could be made with the use of the timpani part.

If it is a multi-movement work, it is conceivable the note-head count for the first movement would be made with the use of the snare drum and the timpani would be used for the second movement—going back to the snare drum part for the third movement.

If there is no visually apparent difference between the snare drum and timpani parts, it might be advantageous to make a note-head count of both parts. For the final reckoning, use the part with the greater number of note-head counts for the composite note-head count.

DoD Work Sheet #5 allows the user to count all the note-heads in measure 1—those for the flute, the clarinet, the saxophone, etc., going "down the score." Then move on to measure 5—going "down the score" again counting the note-heads for the flute, then the clarinet, then the alto saxophone, etc.

FOR FATIGUE FACTOR COMPONENT #4— CONDIMENT COUNT

42. Using another *DoD* Work Sheet #5—with a check mark for the Condiment Count.

Like the note-head count, the musical condiment count will also be a sample count, i.e., not all the condiments to be performed by all the instruments will be counted.

Musical condiments include any written directions that change or enhance the methods of execution or performance of a tone, a series of tones, or section of a composition.

There are four categories of condiments to consider. They include:

1. Any type of articulation specification like staccato, sempre staccato, slurred-staccato, tenuto, accent, etc. Slurs are counted as condiments, but note a tie.

2. Any stylistic indications like marcato, dolce, cantable, et al.

3. Accidentals are to be counted as condiments. Any accidental that appears in a survey measure is to be counted in this category. If the composition is in the key of B-flat and there is a B-natural in the measure, that B-natural is to be counted as a condiment. If there are two B-flats in the measure, two condiments would be counted.

4. Any indication that indicates a tempo change like rit., accel., rall., fermata, caesura, or if the measure being counted calls for a change from Allegro to Andante, that change is counted as a condiment.

Note: When counting condiments, take care to note the appearances of "simile" where such things as staccato are continuous. For example: if a "simile" appears in measure 18, in order to continue a passage of staccato into measure 21, measure 20 would have each note to be performed staccato as a separate condiment.

Illustrations 2 through 5 show how some condiments are to be counted. For purposes of the illustration, the measures here are measures number 9, 10, and 11.

Illustration 2

This measure number 10 would be counted as having six condiments, i.e.,

1 for the accent
1 for the slur
1 for the accent
2 for the staccato indications
1 for the crescendo that started in measure
9 that continued through measure 10

If measure 10 had appeared as Illustration 34, the condiment count would be 3.

Illustration 4 would be counted as having zero condiments.

Illustration 3   **Illustration 4**

This is assuming there was no earlier indication like marcato that would apply to this measure or poco-a-poco-accel., et al. If an accelerando had begun in measure 8 and culminated in measure 12, that measure 10 in Illustration 35 would be given a condiment count of 1.

Illustration 5 would contain 7 condiment counts.

Illustration 5

1 for the breath mark
1 for the fermata over the half note
1 for the fermata over the quarter rest
2 for the forte-piano indicator
1 for the crescendo
1 for the fortissimo indicator

If the note-head count was deleted for the snare drum, delete that instrument here also. If the timpani part was used for the note-head count for a particular composition or movement, use that same part for the condiment count.

43. Using another *DoD* Work Sheet #6, secure the composite condiment count.

44. Enter the condiment count for each instrument on *DoD* Work Sheet #6 on the appropriate lines.

45. Add the counts for each individual instrument together and divide by seven (as indicated). This provides the composite condiment count.

If there was no condiment count for snare drum, divide the total of the six other instruments by six—as with the note-head count.

FOR SECURING THE COMPOSITE FATIGUE FACTOR

46. Using *DoD* Work Sheet #7, secure a composite fatigue factor.

47. Enter each of the four fatigue factor components on the appropriate lines and add those four components together to arrive at the composite fatigue factor.

48. Compare the composite fatigue factor with the *P-DoD-V* levels given at the bottom of that Work Sheet—the Conversion Chart.

FOR CATEGORY G—INSTRUMENTATION

49. With the use of the instrumentation ingredients found on page 132, select the most appropriate *P-DoD-V* (Partial *DoD* Value) and enter that figure on the appropriate line of *DoD* Work Sheet #8—Final Outcomes.

FOR SECURING THE FINAL OUTCOME

50. Using *DoD* Work Sheet #8, secure the final *DoD* outcome.

51. Add the individual Partial *DoD* Factors together, divide by seven (as indicated) to arrive at the *DoD* for the composition.

52. Using the correlation chart, convert the *P-DoD-V* into the *DoD* for the composition. For instance, if the Partial *DoD* Factors averaged out to be 4.35, the *DoD* for the composition in question would be -5. If the Partial *DoD* Factors averaged out to be 1.82, the *DoD* for the composition in question would be -1, etc.

INGREDIENTS FOR CATEGORY A—KEY SIGNATURES
Concert Key
including relative minors

Major keys of B♭, F	= P-DoD-V:1
Major keys of C, E♭	= P-DoD-V:2
Major keys of A♭, G	= P-DoD-V:3
Major keys of D, A	= P-Dod-V:4
Major keys of E, B	= P-DoD-V:5
Major keys of F♯, C♯	= P-DoD-V:6

INGREDIENTS FOR CATEGORY B—METER SIGNATURES*

2/3, 3/4, 4/4, C	= P-DoD-V:1
2/2, 3/2, 4/2, alla breve, 2/8, 3/8, 4/8	= P-DoD-V:2
5/4, 7/4, 6/4, 9/4, 12/4, 6/8, 9/8, 12/8	= P-DoD-V:3
Infrequent changes, 6/16, 9/16, 12/16	= P-DoD-V:4
Frequent changes	= P-DoD-V:5
Superimposed	= P-DoD-V:6

INGREDIENTS FOR CATEGORY C—TEMPO

Moderato	= P-DoD-V:1
Andante, Allegretto	= P-DoD-V:2
Lento, Allegro	= P-DoD-V:3
Adagio, Vivace	= P-DoD-V:4
Largo, Presto	= P-DoD-V:5
Grave, Prestissimo	= P-DoD-V:6

*Based on the research of Duane E. Wareham for D.Ed. dissertation at Pennsylvania State University, 1967, THE DEVELOPMENT AND EVALUATION OF OBJECTIVE CRITERIA FOR GRADING BAND MUSIC INTO SIX LEVELS OF DIFFICULTY, Ann Arbor, Michigan, University Microfilms, Inc., 1982.

INGREDIENTS FOR CATEGORY D—RHYTHM PATTERNS*
P-DoD-V:1

1. Division of the beat into two equal parts using simple meters only, e.g., 2/4, 3/4, and 4/4 (C)
2. All combinations of whole, half, quarter, dotted-quarter, and eighth notes except for those combinations which would create syncopation.
3. All combinations of whole, half, quarter, and eighth rests except those which would create syncopation.

Examples:

*Original material from Duane E. Wareham, D.Ed., dissertation at Pennsylvania State University, 1967, THE DEVELOPMENT AND EVALUATION OF OBJECTIVE CRITERIA FOR GRADING BAND MUSIC INTO SIX LEVELS OF DIFFICULTY, Ann Arbor, Michigan, University Microfilms, Inc., 1982.

INGREDIENTS FOR CATEGORY D—RHYTHM PATTERNS*
P-DoD-V:2

Includes all the rhythm patterns employed in *P-DoD-V*:1 plus the following:

1. Division of the beat into four equal parts using *alla breve*.
2. Simple meters used exclusively with the addition of C or 2/2, 3/2, 4/2, 2/8, 3/8, and 4/8.
3. Sixteenth notes introduced but their use limited to the dotted-eighth and sixteenth rhythm.
4. No syncopation except for simple syncopation.
5. All combinations of the above rhythms except those which would create syncopation.

Examples include:

*Original material from Duane E. Wareham, D.Ed., dissertation at Pennsylvania State University, 1967, THE DEVELOPMENT AND EVALUATION OF OBJECTIVE CRITERIA FOR GRADING BAND MUSIC INTO SIX LEVELS OF DIFFICULTY, Ann Arbor, Michigan, University Microfilms, Inc., 1982.

INGREDIENTS FOR CATEGORY D—RHYTHM PATTERNS
P-DoD-V:3

Includes all the rhythm patterns employed in *P-DoD-V*:1 and 2 plus the following:

1. Division of the beat into three equal parts.
2. Compound and irregular meters introduced.
3. Grace notes introduced.
4. Sixteenth notes limited and used sparingly.
5. Syncopation introduced and limited to the accent of a weak beat and the weak part of a divided beat.
6. All combinations of the above rhythms except for the use of sixteenth notes. Do not break sixteenth groups, except for dotted-eight and sixteenth, and use sixteenth groups sparingly.

Examples:

INGREDIENTS FOR CATEGORY D—RHYTHM PATTERNS
P-DoD-V:4

Includes all the rhythm patterns employed in *P-DoD-V*:1, 2, and 3 plus the following:

1. Division of the beat into six equal parts.
2. Sixteenth notes used frequently in groups and in combinations with eighth notes.
3. Introduction of the fugue.
4. More frequent use of the tie to create syncopation and to extend rhythmic patterns beyond bar lines.

Examples:

INGREDIENTS FOR CATEGORY D—RHYTHM PATTERNS
P-DoD-V:5

Includes all the rhythm patterns employed in *P-DoD-V*:1, 2, 3, and 4 plus the following:

1. Division of the beat into five, seven, and eight or more parts.
2. Compound division of the beat in simple time and the simple division of the beat in compound time.
3. Syncopation within the subdivided beat.
4. Trill introduced.

Examples:

CATEGORY E—RHYTHM PATTERNS FOR *P-DoD-V:6*

Includes all the rhythm patterns employed in *P-DoD-V*:1, 2, 3, 4, and 5 plus unlimited resources in rhythmic combinations.

INGREDIENTS FOR CATEGORY E—INSTRUMENT RANGE

The range of the instruments given are in terms of staffless notation. For reference purposes, the following is the staffless notation system to be used.

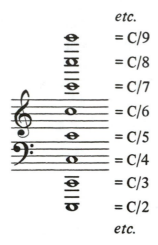

Staffless notation is designated as follows: "Middle C" is designated as C/5. The *D* just above that (the first space below the treble staff) would be designated as D/5. Likewise, the first line of the treble staff would be designated as E/5. The fifth line of the treble staff would be designated as F/6. The fifth line of the bass staff would be designated as A/4, etc.

Flute:	E/5 to G/6	= *P-DoD-V*:1
	E/5 to C/7	= *P-DoD-V*:2
	E/5 to E/7	= *P-DoD-V*:3
	D/5 to F/7	= *P-DoD-V*:4
	D/5 to G/7	= *P-DoD-V*:5
	C/5 to C/8	= *P-DoD-V*:6

Oboe:	E/5 to G/6	= *P-DoD-V*:1
	E/5 to Bb/6	= *P-DoD-V*:2
	E/5 to C/7	= *P-DoD-V*:3
	D/5 to C/7	= *P-DoD-V*:4
	C/5 to E/7	= *P-DoD-V*:5
	B/4 to C/7	= *P-DoD-V*:6

Clarinet:	G/4 to G/7	= *P-DoD-V*:1
	G/4 to Bb/7	= *P-DoD-V*:2
	F/4 to C/8	= *P-DoD-V*:3
	E/4 to E/8	= *P-DoD-V*:4
	E/4 to F/8	= *P-DoD-V*:5
	E/4 to A/8	= *P-DoD-V*:6

Saxophone:	E/5 to G/6	= *P-DoD-V*:1
	D/5 to B/6	= *P-DoD-V*:2
	D/5 to C/7	= *P-DoD-V*:3
	D/5 to D/7	= *P-DoD-V*:4
	C/5 to E/7	= *P-DoD-V*:5
	Bb/4 to F/7	= *P-DoD-V*:6

Bassoon:	F/3 to Bb/4	= *P-DoD-V*:1
	E/3 to D/3	= *P-DoD-V*:2
	C/3 to E/5	= *P-DoD-V*:3
	B/2 to F/5	= *P-DoD-V*:4
	Bb/2 to G/5	= *P-DoD-V*:5
	Bb/2 to Bb/5	= *P-DoD-V*:6

Cornet:	C/5 to C/6	= *P-DoD-V*:1
	C/5 to E/6	= *P-DoD-V*:2
	Bb/4 to G/6	= *P-DoD-V*:3
	A/4 to A/6	= *P-DoD-V*:4
	G/4 to Bb/7	= *P-DoD-V*:5
	F#/4 to C/7	= *P-DoD-V*:6

French horn:	C/5 to C/6	= *P-DoD-V*:1
	B/4 to D/6	= *P-DoD-V*:2
	A/4 to E/6	= *P-DoD-V*:3
	G/4 to G/6	= *P-DoD-V*:4
	F/4 to G/6	= *P-DoD-V*:5
	F/4 to A/6	= *P-DoD-V*:6

Trombone:	Bb/3 to Bb/4	= *P-DoD-V*:1
	Bb/3 to D/5	= *P-DoD-V*:2
	G/3 to D/5	= *P-DoD-V*:3
	G/3 to E/5	= *P-DoD-V*:4
	F/3 to F/5	= *P-DoD-V*:5
	F/3 to A/5	= *P-DoD-V*:6

Baritone horn:	C/5 to C/6	= *P-DoD-V*:1
	C/5 to E/6	= *P-DoD-V*:2
	Bb/4 to G/6	= *P-DoD-V*:3
	A/4 to A/6	= *P-DoD-V*:4
	G/4 to Bb/7	= *P-DoD-V*:5
	F#/4 to C/7	= *P-DoD-V*:6

Tuba:	Bb/2 to Bb/3	= *P-DoD-V*:1
	Ab/2 to Bb/3	= *P-DoD-V*:2
	Ab/2 to Eb/3	= *P-DoD-V*:3
	G/2 to G/4	= *P-DoD-V*:4
	F/2 to A/4	= *P-DoD-V*:5
	E/2 to Bb/4	= *P-DoD-V*:6

131

INGREDIENTS FOR CATEGORY G—INSTRUMENTATION

If the composition calls for a minimum of instrumentation and all portions of the composition are generally played in tutti. . . .

= *P-DoD-V*:1

If the composition calls for a minimum of instrumentation but there are some sectionally individual soli passages. . . .

= *P-DoD-V*:2

If the composition calls for full instrumentation and tutti playing, soli parts within sections, and solos are cross-cued. . . .

= *P-DoD-V*:3

If the composition calls for full instrumentation with few alternate cues, occasional soli and solo passages. . . .

= *P-DoD-V*:4

If the composition calls for the maximum of instrumentation, isolated solo passages and a minimum of cross-cues. . . .

= *P-DoD-V*:5

If the composition calls for the maximum of instrumentation, open voicings, isolated solos and soli passages. . . .

= *P-DoD-V*:6

DoD Work Sheet #1
CATEGORIES A THROUGH D

COMPOSITION _____

Category A—The key signature(s) include:

P-DoD-V: _____

Category B—The meter signature(s) include:

P-DoD-V: _____

Category C—The tempi include:

P-DoD-V: _____

Category D—The rhythm patterns include:

P-DoD-V: _____

DoD Work Sheet #2
CATEGORY E—INSTRUMENT RANGE

COMPOSITION: _____

Flute _____ P-DoD-V: _____

Oboe _____ P-DoD-V: _____

Clarinet _____ P-DoD-V: _____

Saxophone _____ P-DoD-V: _____

Bassoon _____ P-DoD-V: _____

Cornet _____ P-DoD-V: _____

French Horn _____ P-Dod-V: _____

Trombone _____ P-DoD-V: _____

Baritone Horn _____ P-DoD-V: _____

Tuba _____ P-DoD-V: _____

The average *DoD* for Category G is *P-DoD-V:* _____

DoD Work Sheet #3
Category F — Fatigue Factor

FFC #1 — Performance Time
FF #1 through FF #5

COMPOSITION _____

Sec.	Meter Count FF #1	X	Number of Meas. FF #2	=	Gross Meter Count FF #3	:	Metronome Setting FF #4	=	Sec. Time Factor FF #5
A		X		=		:		=	
B		X		=		:		=	
C		X		=		:		=	
D		X		=		:		=	
E		X		=		:		=	
F		X		=		:		=	
G		X		=		:		=	
H		X		=		:		=	
J		X		=		:		=	
K		X		=		:		=	
L		X		=		:		=	
M		X		=		:		=	
N		X		=		:		=	
P		X		=		:		=	
Q		X		=		:		=	
R		X		=		:		=	
S		X		=		:		=	
T		X		=		:		=	
U		X		=		:		=	
V		X		=		:		=	
W		X		=		:		=	
X		X		=		:		=	
Y		X		=		:		=	
Z		X		=		:		=	

Total Sec. Time Factors: _____ X 60 = Numerical Time Factor: _____

DoD Work Sheet #4
Category F — Fatigue Factor

FFC #2 — Metronomic Counts

COMPOSITION _____

Box 1 is for the Meter Count
Box 2 is for the Number of Measures
Box 3 becomes the Sectional Metronomic Count

	Box 1		Box 2		Box 3			Box 1		Box 2		Box 3
MC-1		X		=			MC-2		X		=	
MC-3		X		=			MC-4		X		=	
MC-5		X		=			MC-6		X		=	
MC-7		X		=			MC-8		X		=	
MC-9		X		=			MC-10		X		=	
MC-11		X		=			MC-12		X		=	
MC-13		X		=			MC-14		X		=	
MC-15		X		=			MC-16		X		=	
MC-17		X		=			MC-18		X		=	
MC-19		X		=			MC-20		X		=	

TOTAL METRONOMIC COUNT (FFC #2): _____

DoD Work Sheet #5

COMPOSITION _____

☐ Note-Head Count   ☐ Condiment Count

m.	Fl	Cl	Sx	Cr	Hn	Tb	Sn
1							
5							
10							
15							
20							
25							
30							
35							
40							
45							
50							
55							
60							
65							
70							
75							
80							
85							
90							
95							
100							
105							
110							
115							
120							
125							
130							
135							
140							
145							

DoD Work Sheet #5—page 2

COMPOSITION _____

☐ Note-Head Count   ☐ Condiment Count

m.	Fl	Cl	Sx	Cr	Hn	Tb	Sn
150							
155							
160							
165							
170							
175							
180							
185							
190							
195							
200							
205							
210							
215							
220							
225							
230							
235							
240							
245							
250							
255							
260							
265							
270							
275							
280							
285							
290							
295							
300							

DoD Work Sheet #6
Category F—Fatigue Factor

☐ **FFC #3—Composite Note-Head Count**
☐ **FFC #4—Composite Condiment Count**

COMPOSITION _____

Total Count for

1st Flute . . . .   ———

1st Clarinet . . . .   ———

1st Alto Saxophone . . . .   ———

1st Cornet . . . .   ———

1st French Horn . . . .   ———

1st Trombone . . . .   ———

Snare Drum . . . .   ———

TOTAL   ———

DIVIDE BY   7

EQUALS THE NOTE-HEAD COUNT (FFC #3)   ———

DoD Work Sheet #7
Category F—Composite Fatigue Factor

COMPOSITION _____

Total of

FFC #1—Performance Time .... _____

FFC #2—Metronomic Count .... _____

FFC #3—Note-Head Count .... _____

FFC #4—Condiment Count .... _____

TOTAL FATIGUE FACTOR (CATEGORY F)   _____

Conversion Chart

299 or less = *P-DoD-V:*1

300 to 474 = *P-DoD-V:*2

475 to 674 = *P-DoD-V:*3

675 to 924 = *P-DoD-V:*4

925 to 1199 = *P-DoD-V:*5

1200 or more = *P-DoD-V:*6

DoD Work Sheet #8
Final Outcome

COMPOSITION _____

Category A—Key Signature .... *P-DoD-V:* _____
Category B—Meter Signature .... *P-DoD-V:* _____
Category C—Tempi .... *P-DoD-V:* _____
Category D—Rhythm Patterns .... *P-DoD-V:* _____
Cateogry E—Instrument Range .... *P-DoD-V:* _____
Category F—Fatigue Factor .... *P-DoD-V:* _____
Category G—Instrumentation .... *P-DoD-V:* _____

TOTAL   _____

DIVIDE BY   _7_

Equals the average *P-DoD-V*   _____

Correlation Chart to Convert P-DoD-V into Dod

1.00 to 1.83 = *DoD*-1
1.84 to 2.67 = *DoD*-2
2.68 to 3.50 = *DoD*-3
3.51 to 4.33 = *DoD*-4
4.34 to 5.17 = *DoD*-5
5.18 to 6.00 = *DoD*-6

Thus this composition is rated as *DoD*- _____

CRITERION MODEL #5

EVALUATING PRIVATE LESSONS

Place a checkmark in the appropriate box.

as needed or always
almost always
sometimes
seldom, if ever

INSTRUCTIONAL SYSTEMATIZATION

□ □ □ □ 1. Gives explicit instructions regarding what materials are to be practiced.

□ □ □ □ 2. Discusses what goals should be achieved during practice sessions.

□ □ □ □ 3. Music that is chosen is designed to increase musical abilities and/or technical competencies.

□ □ □ □ 4. Supplementary materials are used to augment and/or reinforce learning.

□ □ □ □ 5. Reference materials are used and/or given or suggested to further understandings.

□ □ □ □ 6. When a new composition is given, help is offered so there is an understanding of what is to be accomplished or how the composition is to be approached.

INSTRUCTIONAL SKILLS

□ □ □ □ 7. Explanations are clear and concise.

□ □ □ □ 8. Instructions are at the level of the students' proficiencies.

□ □ □ □ 9. As a part of the lesson, technical problems are diagnosed.

□ □ □ □ 10. Once problems are diagnosed, steps are given to help alleviate the deficiency.

□ □ □ □ 11. The teacher is persistent in seeing that technical problems are overcome or at least what needs to be done to overcome them is understood.

GENERAL INSTRUCTIONAL CONSIDERATIONS

□ □ □ □ 12. Is willing to admit mistakes.

□ □ □ □ 13. Teaching includes criticism and correction mixed with compliments and praise.

□ □ □ □ 14. Communicates ideas clearly.

□ □ □ □ 15. Relates to a sense of responsibility which is needed to get the work done.

□ □ □ □ 16. Has an accurate perception of student's ability.

□ □ □ □ 17. Communicates on student's level, i.e., does not "talk down" to the student.

□ □ □ □ 18. Shows the attitude of stick-to-it-iveness.

RAPPORT

□ □ □ □ 19. Instills a feeling of confidence.

□ □ □ □ 20. Encourages the student to express him- or herself.

□ □ □ □ 21. Brings out the best in the student.

□ □ □ □ 22. Shows genuine interest in the student outside the lesson.

□ □ □ □ 23. Is patient and understanding.

CRITERION MODEL #6

EVALUATING CLASS LESSONS*

Place a checkmark in the appropriate box.

as needed or always	almost always	sometimes	seldom, if ever	
				INSTRUCTIONAL SYSTEMATIZATION
☐	☐	☐	☐	1. Gives explicit instructions regarding what materials are to be practiced.
☐	☐	☐	☐	2. Discusses what goals should be achieved during practice sessions.
☐	☐	☐	☐	3. Music that is chosen is designed to increase musical abilities and/or technical competencies.
☐	☐	☐	☐	4. Supplementary materials are used to augment and/or reinforce learning.
☐	☐	☐	☐	5. Reference materials are used and/or given or suggested to further understandings.
☐	☐	☐	☐	6. When a new composition is given, help is offered to give an understanding of what is to be accomplished or how the composition is to be approached.
				INSTRUCTIONAL SKILLS
☐	☐	☐	☐	7. Considerations are given for individual differences.
☐	☐	☐	☐	8. Explanations are clear and concise.
☐	☐	☐	☐	9. Instructions are at the level of the students' proficiencies.
☐	☐	☐	☐	10. As a part of the lesson, technical problems are diagnosed.
☐	☐	☐	☐	11. Once problems are diagnosed, steps are given to help alleviate the deficiency.
☐	☐	☐	☐	12. The teacher is persistent in seeing that technical problems are overcome or at least in explaining what needs to be done to overcome them.
				GENERAL INSTRUCTIONAL CONSIDERATIONS
☐	☐	☐	☐	13. Is willing to admit mistakes.
☐	☐	☐	☐	14. Teaching includes criticism and correction mixed with compliments and praise.
☐	☐	☐	☐	15. Communicates ideas clearly.
☐	☐	☐	☐	16. Relates to a sense of responsibility which is needed to get the work done.
☐	☐	☐	☐	17. Has an accurate perception of student's ability.
☐	☐	☐	☐	18. Communicates on student's level, i.e., does not "talk down" to the student.
☐	☐	☐	☐	19. Shows the attitude of stick-to-it-iveness.

*H.F. Abeles, "Student Perceptions of Characteristics of Effective Applied Music Instructors." JOURNAL OF RESEARCH IN MUSIC EDUCATION, 23, 2 (Summer 1975), 147.

as needed or always	almost always	sometimes	seldom, if ever	

RAPPORT

□	□	□	□	20. Instills a feeling of confidence.
□	□	□	□	21. Encourages the student to express him- or herself.
□	□	□	□	22. Brings out the best in the student.
□	□	□	□	23. Shows genuine interest in the student outside the lesson.
□	□	□	□	24. Is patient and understanding.

CLASS ROUTINE

□	□	□	□	25. Interclass discussions are fostered to reinforce learning concepts.
□	□	□	□	26. Performance demonstrations by individual class members cre used to reinforce performance concepts.
□	□	□	□	27. Intraclass competition is encouraged but only for purposes of learning the materials or reinforcing learning concepts.
□	□	□	□	28. Opportunity is given for individual performance within the class sessions.
□	□	□	□	29. No partiality is shown to any one class member.

CRITERION MODEL #7

EVALUATING STAGE BAND REHEARSALS

Evaluate each item in the criteria using the following standards.

E—if the provision or condition is made extensively
S—if the provision or condition is made to some extent
L—if the provision or condition is limited
V—if the provision or condition is very limited
M—if the provision or condition is missing and needed
N—if the provision or condition does not apply or is not necessarily desirable

If a final outcome is desired, consult the steps given in Criterion Model #1.

TECHNICAL FACTORS

_____ **1. Is the band phrasing and articulating in a proper, idiomatic manner?**

_____ a. Are they slurring (the slur in the classical sense is never used)?

_____ b. Are they articulating each note with a legato articulation of some kind?

_____ c. Are they avoiding the hard, explosive "tut" attack?

_____ d. Are they ending releases or final eighth notes or separated quarter notes with the tongue in a crisp manner (*duht*)?

_____ e. Are they maintaining a constant, driving air-flow under connected notes in a phrase?

_____ f. Are they separating notes only when phrase determinations indicate this?

_____ g. Are they observing idiomatic articulation and phrase differences between swing and rock; between up-tempo and ballads?

_____ **2. Is the band accenting in the proper manner?**

_____ a. Do they realize the syncopation or "off-beat" nature of jazz?

_____ b. Are they pushing on off-beats?

_____ c. Are they accenting the syncopated release notes of a phrase (the most important notes)?

_____ **3. Is the band playing with good tone production? There is no real difference between a good jazz sound and good** 'classical' sound. Jazz begins with and builds from a good sound. There is no substitute for technical mastery of the instrument.

_____ a. Are they constantly aware of the sound they are producing; the quality of the entire sound from beginning to end?

_____ b. Are they avoiding excessive (either wide or fast) vibrato?

_____ c. Are they matching vibratos?

_____ d. Are they avoiding the use of vibrato in unison passages?

_____ e. Are they aware of the techniques of varying the speed and intensity of vibrato?

_____ f. Are they overblowing, 'blatting?'

_____ g. Are they breathing in the proper manner?

_____ h. Are they using enough breath and supporting each tone they produce, especially in the changes from note to note where no separation can exist?

_____ **4. Is the band listening to each other in order to establish the proper balance?**

_____ a. Do the outside players 'play up' to the lead players in the sections?

_____ b. Do you clearly hear all of the notes in the written harmonies?

_____ c. Do the sections listen to each other and balance each other?

_____ d. Do all players in full band ensembles listen to the lead trumpet and follow his phrasing?

_____ e. Is the rhythm section too loud to balance the rest of the band, especially in 'rock' or amplified music?

_____ f. Is each member of the band aware of what the rest of the players are doing and of his own part at every moment?

_____ g. Do they listen? Really listen?

_____ **5. Is the band playing with good intonation?**

_____ a. Are they listening to each other to favor notes into tune?

_____ b. Are they aware of notes that must be favored on their instruments?

_____ c. Are they aware of the sound of the choral harmonies of an ensemble part?

_____ d. Are they especially critical in the danger spots: unisons, and 'bad notes' on their particular instruments?

_____ e. Are they particularly aware of intonation problems in pianissimo passages where a lack of proper air support can be critical; in crescendos and dimunuendos?

_____   **6. Is the band playing with dynamics?**

_____   a. Do they appreciate the full spectrum of dynamics from *ppp* to *fff*?

_____   b. Do they ever play really soft?

_____   c. Can they terrace dynamics effectively with a balance in all parts?

_____   d. Can they diminuendo and crescendo gradually and evenly while maintaining a balance of parts?

_____   e. Do all of your performances vary the dynamics levels, i.e., tend not to be too loud in a monotonous, hammering way?

_____   f. Does the rhythm section, especially the drums and amplified instruments, vary the dynamics as much as the horns?

_____   g. Are they aware of the effectiveness and impact of the subito piano or of exaggerated dynamics in both directions?

_____   **7. Is the band playing with a good, consistent sense of rhythm or time?**

_____   a. Is the rhythmic pulse steady?

_____   b. Are all members of the band aware of the beat?

_____   c. Do all members of the band maintain the pulse as a driving thing within themselves?

_____   d. Is the rhythmic feeling correct for the style of music being performed?

_____   e. If you are doing 'rock,' are you doing it correctly?

_____   f. Is the band aware that there are very definite rhythmic modes that vary from tune to tune and style to style?

_____   g. Is your choice of tempo correct?

_____   h. Is the band aware of the function of 'kick' and 'lift' notes?

_____   i. Are they playing rests rhythmically?

_____   j. Are they aware of the function of the 'crisp' release' in propelling the rhythmic feeling?

_____   k. Are they maintaining accurate rhythm on consecutive quarter notes, i.e., not rushing consecutive quarter notes, especially on beats two and four?

_____   l. In 'swing' arrangements, are they aware of the beat division and holding back on off-beat eighth notes?

_____   m. Can they 'lay-back' on strings of consecutive quarter notes or syncopated quarter note values?

_____   n. Is the rhythm section stretching out and playing in a more linear manner i.e., not playing in a 'boxy' manner with a disconcerted vertical feel?

———— 8. **Is the band performing (or rehearsing) the music in a manner that communicates and excites the band itself and the audience?**

———— a. Are the students involved in the music they are playing?

———— b. Do they generate a rhythmic, dynamic, melodic excitement in their performance?

———— c. Do they sit 'on the end of their chairs' or like so many 'lumps' playing correct notes while the music passes them by (maybe the director should examine the music he is programming for value and viability)?

———— 9. **Is the band aware of the basics of musical aesthetics?**

———— a. Are they aware of the constant need for and role of tension and release in all music?

———— b. Do they grasp the musical implications of their parts?

———— c. Are they able to identify the musical function of the line or part they are playing? Is it the melody; background; rhythmic pulse; etc.

———— d. Are they constantly aware of the direction in which their phrase is going—is it building tension; is it at the point of release?

———— e. Can they identify the most important note(s) in their phrase?

———— f. Can they visualize the overall form and impact of a composition, or are they limited in their perception to the individual notes they are playing?

UNIVERSALITY AND AUTHENTICITY

———— 1. **Are the band members exposed to all forms of music even though a particular style of jazz may not be their favorite?**

———— a. Is the music and style of Count Basie, Stan Kenton, Buddy Rich, and Don Ellis performed? How about free-form and avant-garde, ballads, medium and up-tempo, swing, jazz-rock, rock, or modern swing (Oliver Nelson, Thad Jones)?

———— 2. **Is the band aware of the stylistic differences demanded for a proper idiomatic performance of the various types of music? Can they analyze and define the differences in style?**

———— 3. **Has the band ever heard the different styles of music either live or on recordings?**

———— a. Are they encouraged to listen to jazz in all its forms?

———— b. Do you ever play a recording of the music being performed for the students so they can imitate the proper style of the music?

_____ c. Is there a constant effort made to perform the different styles of music as professionally and as correctly as possible? Are you as director aware of the stylistic differences?

_____ d. Do you constantly correct deviations from the stylistic norms?

IMPROVISATION

_____ **1. Do you stress the necessity of improvisation in your jazz band?**

_____ a. Do you teach improvisation to all members of your band?

_____ b. Are you aware of the various published 'methods' for teaching and developing improvisions?

_____ c. Do you believe that improvision, and not ensemble playing, is the heart of the jazz band?

_____ **2. Are the students aware of the principles of aesthetics, tension and release, building, and ending that must characterize a solo?**

_____ a. Are they aware of the techniques of solo playing that are peculiar to their instruments?

_____ b. Are they aware of the major jazz performers on their instruments?

_____ c. Do you evaluate the effectiveness and musicality of their solos?

_____ d. Are they aware of their function as soloists in the big band concept?

_____ **3. Are the students building the technical equipment for good improvisation: scales, ear-training, etc.?**

_____ a. Are they aware of the harmonic changes?

_____ b. Do they listen to the rhythm section?

_____ c. Does the rhythm section listen to the soloist and respond to him or her?

_____ **4. Do you demand improvisation? Are the students allowed to play the 'written' solo without even the most elementary efforts at personalization?**

CHOICE OF MUSIC

_____ **1. Is the music that the band is playing suited to the level of musical development within the band, or is it beyond their physical and mental capabilities?**

_____ **2. Is it musically good (there is a tremendous amount of** marginal or worse music ground out each year by the publishers)?

_____ 3. Is the music challenging and interesting to the band; does it stretch them a little to encourage practice and growth?

_____ 4. Do you spend as much time in the evaluation and selection of music for the jazz group as for your concert band? Are you aware of the sources of good arrangements?

_____ 5. Do you attend reading sessions, festivals, or clinics with an evaluative ear to finding new and educationally fulfilling arrangements for your jazz band?

_____ 6. Do you encourage the arranging and composition of music by members of your group?*

*George Wiskirchen, "Rehearsing a School Jazz Band." *Jazz in the 70's—A High School Teacher's Guide* (Elkhart, Indiana: The Selmer Co., 22.)

CRITERION MODEL #8

EVALUATING THE MARCHING BAND
WORK SHEET FOR OUTCOMES

STEP #1: Enter the number of *A* ratings: _____

multiply by 4 = _____

STEP #2: Enter the number of *B* ratings: _____

multiply by 3 = _____

STEP #3: Enter the number of *C* ratings: _____

multiply by 2 = _____

STEP #4: Enter the number of *D* ratings: _____

multiply by 1 _____

STEP #5: Enter the number of *F* ratings: _____

multiply by 0 = __0__

STEP #6: Total all the above _____

STEP #7: Divide the total (Step #6) by 4 = _____

STEP #8: Compare the figure that results from Step #7 with the verbal outcome given below.

3.3 to 4.0 = Excellent
2.5 to 3.2 = Very Good
1.7 to 2.4 = Good
0.9 to 1.6 = Fair
0.0 to 0.8 = Poor

EVALUATING THE MARCHING BAND

On the lines provided, indicate your opinion of how each item is being carried out. The rating scale is as follows (except where otherwise provided):

A = Excellent or at a high degree
B = Very Good or at a considerable degree
C = Good or at an average degree
D = Fair or at a rather low degree
P = Poor or at a very low degree

_____ 1. Charts of formations and procedures are readable.

_____ 2. Charts of formations and procedures are helpful.

_____ 3. Directions that are given for movements make possible an understanding as to what should be done and when.

_____ 4. Verbal directions given by the director(s) are such that they are understandable.

_____ 5. The drum major understands his or her duties and responsibilities

_____ 6. The drum major is helpful in seeing the band meets its duties and responsibilities.

_____ 7. The band's officers act in a responsible fashion.

_____ 8. Staff members act in a responsible fashion.

_____ 9. Section leaders act in a responsible fashion.

_____ 10. Section leaders understand and carry out their duties and responsibilities.

_____ 11. Section leaders are selected appropriately.

_____ 12. Rank leaders act in a responsible fashion.

_____ 13. Rank leaders understand and carry out their duties and responsibilities.

_____ 14. Rank leaders are selected appropriately.

_____ 15. Concerning the number of performances:

A = just right   D = too few
B = could be more   F = too many
C = a few too many

_____ 16. When performances take place:

A = arrangements are always well planned
B = arrangements are almost always well planned

C = arrangements are not too well planned
D = arrangements need to be planned better
E = arrangements are very poorly planned

_____ 17. Performances vs. academic school work:

A = no interference that causes any great amount of
      problems
B = some interference but of no great consequences
C = some interference
D = causes problems with academic school work
F = causes a great deal of problems and interferes too
      much with academic school work.

In the space below, please comment on the following: How can marching band participation be made more beneficial, rewarding and/or enjoyable?

_____

_____

_____

_____

_____

_____

_____

_____

_____

CRITERION MODEL #9

EVALUATING PUBLIC RELATIONS STRATEGIES WORK SHEET FOR OUTCOMES

STEP #1:   Enter the number of *E* ratings: _____

                 multiply by 4 = _____

STEP #2:   Enter the number of *S* ratings: _____

                 multiply by 3 = _____

STEP #3:   Enter the number of *L* ratings: _____

                 multiply by 2 = _____

STEP #4:   Enter the number of *V* ratings: _____

                 multiply by 1 = _____

STEP #5:   Add all the above subtotals and enter here: _____

STEP #6:   Divide the subtotal of Step 5 by the number 4 = _____*

The verbal outcome would be as follows:

> 3.3 to 4.0 = Excellent
> 2.5 to 3.2 = Very Good
> 1.7 to 2.4 = Good
> 0.9 to 1.6 = Fair
> 0.0 to 0.8 = Poor

*This is the numerical outcome.

EVALUATING PUBLIC RELATIONS STRATEGIES

Evaluate each item in the criteria as follows:

E —if the provision or condition is made extensively

S —if the provision or condition is made to some extent

L —if the provision or condition is limited

V —if the provision or condition is very limited

M—if the provision or condition is missing and needed

N—if the provision or condition does not apply or is not necessarily desirable

Kindergarten Classes Are Provided With:

_____ 1. films, filmstrips, and/or videocassettes about bands/orchestras and their instruments.

_____ 2. live performances by elementary, junior, and high school soloists.

_____ 3. live performances by small ensembles within the band/orchestra.

_____ 4. live performances of the elementary, junior high, and high school band/orchestra via school assembly-concerts.

_____ 5. live performances by professional musicians.

_____ 6. library-type materials about band/orchestras and their instruments.

_____ 7. bulletin board displays and/or materials.

Primary Grade Classes Are Provided With:

_____ 8. films, filmstrips, and/or videocassettes about bands/orchestras and their instruments.

_____ 9. live performances by elementary, junior high, and high school soloists.

_____ 10. live performances by small ensembles within the band/orchestra.

_____ 11. live performances of the elementary, junior high, and high school band/orchestra via school assembly-concerts.

_____ 12. live performances by professional musicians.

_____ 13. library-type materials about bands/orchestras and their instruments.

_____ 14. bulletin board displays and/or materials.

Intermediate Grade Classes Are Provided With:

_____ 15. films, filmstrips, and/or videocassettes about bands/orchestras and their instruments.

_____ 16. live performances by elementary, junior high, and high school soloists.

_____ 17. live performances by small ensembles within the band/orchestra.

_____ 18. live performances of the elementary, junior high, and high school band/orchestra via school assembly-concerts.

_____ 19. live performances by professional musicians.

_____ 20. library-type materials about bands/orchestras and their instruments.

_____ 21. bulletin board displays and/or materials.

Junior High School General Population Is Provided With:

_____ 22. live performances of junior high and high school soloists.

_____ 23. live performances by small ensembles within and band/orchestra.

_____ 24. live performances of the junior high and high school band/orchestra via school assembly-concerts.

_____ 25. live performances by professional musicians.

_____ 26. library-type materials about bands/orchestras and their instruments.

_____ 27. bulletin board displays and/or materials.

_____ 28. The junior high band/orchestra director makes contacts with elementary musicians coming to the junior high school.

_____ 29. Articles are regularly submitted to the junior high school newspaper about the junior high school band, its soloists, and ensembles.

High School General School Population Is Provided With:

_____ 30. live performances by high school soloists.

_____ 31. live performances by small ensembles within the band/orchestra.

_____ 32. live performances of the high school band/orchestra via school assembly-concerts.

_____ 33. live performances by professional musicians.

_____ 34. library-type materials about bands/orchestras and their instruments.

_____ 35. bulletin board displays and/or materials

_____ 36. The high school band/orchestra director makes contact with junior high school musicians coming to the high school.

_____ 37. Articles are regularly submitted to the high school newspaper about the activities of the band/orchestra, its soloists, and ensembles.

*This is the numerical outcome.

CRITERION MODEL #10

EVALUATING A PARENT ASSOCIATION

WORK SHEET

Step #1: Count the number of checkmarks (on each evaluation form that is completed).

Step #2: Divide the total number of checkmarks by the number 25.

Note: If more than one person does the evaluation, multiply the number of evaluators by 25. Use that number as the divisor.

Step #3: Compare the results of Step 2 with the verbal outcomes given below.

95 to 100 = an excellent managerial arrangement
84 to 94 = a very good managerial arrangement
68 to 83 = a good managerial arrangement
42 to 67 = a fair managerial arrangement
 0 to 41 = a poor managerial arrangement

EVALUATING A PARENT ASSOCIATION

Place a checkmark in the box in front of each item that is part of a document setting the guidelines for the Parent Association. This document is most likely the Association's Bylaws.

☐ 1. The membership of the association is restricted to parents of students registered in the band/orchestra.

☐ 2. The band/orchestra director is an official, voting member of the association and its executive board.

☐ 3. The school principal or a representative of such is an official voting member of the association and its executive board.

☐ 4. The lines of authority are clearly defined in the bylaws of the association.

☐ 5. The bylaws clearly state the final authority for activities (when deemed in question) is vested with the school's administration (and its lawyer).

☐ 6. The association and its meetings are governed by *Demeter's Manual of Parliamentary Law and Procedures.*

☐ 7. The purposes of the association are clearly defined in writing.

☐ 8. The activities of the association are aimed at increasing parental knowledge of the instrumental music program and its educational needs.

☐ 9. The association assists with the internal public relations program of the band/orchestra.

☐ 10. The association assists with the external public relations program of the band/orchestra.

☐ 11. The election of officers is governed by the bylaws.

☐ 12. The bylaws call for a systematic method for nomination of officers.

☐ 13. The bylaws call for secret ballot for election of officers.

☐ 14. The duties of the officers are governed by the bylaws.

☐ 15. Provisions are made for periodic review of the bylaws.

☐ 16. The term of office for the officers is governed by the bylaws.

☐ 17. Provisions are made in the bylaws for the eventuality of a child dropping out of the band/orchestra and how it relates to the parent's membership in the association and that of holding or retaining an office.

☐ 18. An executive board is provided for.

☐ 19. The duties and powers of the executive board are clearly defined in the bylaws.

☐ 20. A portion of each general meeting is often devoted to a student showcase.

☐ 21. A portion of each general meeting is devoted to some kind of educational endeavour.

☐ 22. Some kind of newsletter or other means of written communication is provided for.

☐ 23. This communication medium (if only the minutes of the meetings) is distributed to interested school administration officials.

☐ 24. Fund raising sponsored by the association is a minor activity, i.e., takes very little of the executive board's and general meeting's time.

☐ 25. Fund raisers proposed by the association are carried on exclusively by the parents, i.e., not foisted upon the students.

CRITERION MODEL #11

PARENT PRIORITIES

WORK SHEET

Step #1: Record each priority number given for each item of the "Parent Priority" forms on the chart below using the virgule-count-marking system. Use the five-cluster-count-mark for each recorded evaluation code, i.e., one mark in each appropriate box for each evaluation given. For every fifth count, use a cross bar rather than a fifth virgule, i.e., **⊬⊬⊔** . (This helps with arriving at an accurate final count.) For example, if the form in hand has question number 1 as a priority 2, enter a virgule-count-mark in the "Priority 2" column on the "Question #1" line. If question number 2 is rated as Priority 3, place a virgule-count-mark in the "Priority 3" column on the line number 2.

Continue through to question number 17 in like fashion. Do the same with all the completed "Parent Priority" forms.

Step #2: Establish gross priority values as shown in the following example:

QUES.	PRIORITIES					GROSS PRIORITY VALUES
	1	2	3	4	5	
#1						

Step #2a: Count the number of virgules in each priority column for each question.

Step #2b: Multiply the number of virgules in each priority column by the priority number. Place the sum (the number of virgules multiplied by the priority number) in the lower right corner of each respective grid box. Notice in the example there are six marks in the Priority 2 column. These six marks are multiplied by 2. The sum (12) is entered in that lower corner of the grid box. In like fashion, the two virgules in Priority 3 column are multiplied by 3 and entered in that corner of the grid box.

Priority 4 column has five counts times four for a subtotal of twenty. Priority 5 has two virgules for a gross priority value subtotal of ten.

Step #3: Add the numbers in the lower right corners to arrive at a gross priority value for each question. In the example given, the gross priority value for Question X is 51.

Step #4: A final priority list can now be established. The question with the lowest gross priority value becomes the highest priority. The question with the next lowest gross priority value becomes the second highest priority, etc.

PARENT PRIORITIES—SCORING SHEET

QUES.	PRIORITIES 1	2	3	4	5	GROSS PRIORITY VALUES
#1						
#2						
#3						
#4						
#5						
#6						
#7						
#8						
#9						
#10						
#11						
#12						
#13						
#14						
#15						
#16						
#17						

PARENT PRIORITIES

Below is a checklist of various items in the area of parent association activities. Give each item a priority number. Priority 1 would be the highest priority. Priority 5 would be the lowest. More than one item can be given a Priority 1. However, use this priority level sparingly—not more than three or four times. If an item is of no importance or does not apply, put a line across the space for the priority rating.

    ————— 1. Revise bylaws.

    ————— 2. Have more open meetings.

    ————— 3. Provide more membership contacts.

    ————— 4. Provide periodic musical performances at meetings.

    ————— 5. Provide regular musical performances at meetings.

    ————— 6. Provide periodic discussions about the music program.

    ————— 7. Provide regular discussions about the music program.

    ————— 8. Provide more planning for fund raisers.

    ————— 9. Provide more external public relations.

    ————— 10. Provide liaison with the P.T.A.

    ————— 11. Provide more contacts with the school administration.

    ————— 12. Provide demonstration lessons during meetings.

    ————— 13. Provide more input during general meetings from the executive board.

    ————— 14. Provide more input from the general membership to the executive board.

    ————— 15. Provide more controls over spending of association funds.

    ————— 16. Provide more controls on fund raisers.

    ————— 17. Provide more information about executive board meetings and activities.

In the space below, comment on any aspect of the association activities you would like to bring to the attention of those in charge.

_____

_____

_____

_____

_____

CRITERION MODEL #12

PARENT EVALUATION of the INSTRUMENTAL MUSIC PROGRAM

Step #1: Enter one virgule in the appropriate grid box for each evaluation level given to each item. For the "virgule-count-marking system" *see* Criterion Model #13, Step 1.

Step #2: Total the number of virgules in each column and enter that figure in the "Total Virg." (Virgules) box at the bottom of each column.

Step #3: Transfer those individual subtotals to the appropriate slots on the "Numerical Outcomes Formula."

Step #4: Do the multiplication as shown. Multiply the total number of virgules in the "Excellent" box by four, the total number of virgules in the "Very Good" box by three, etc.

Step #5: Add all three subtotal values to get the "Total Values."

Step #6: Divide the total values of the virgules by the total number of virgules. This becomes the numerical outcome.

Step #7: That numerical outcome can then be converted via the chart for "Conversion of Numerical Outcome to a Verbal Outcome."

Numerical Outcome Formula

Number of "Excellent" virgules	_____	× 4	=	_____
Number of "Very Good" virgules	_____	× 3	=	_____
Number of "Good" virgules	_____	× 2	=	_____
Number of "Fair" virgules	_____	× 1	=	_____
Number of "Poor" virgules	_____	× 0	=	0
		TOTAL VALUES	=	_____
	DIVIDED BY TOTAL NUMBER OF VIRGULES			_____
	FINAL OUTCOME			_____

Conversion of Numerical Outcomes to Verbal Outcome

96 to 100 = excellent program
84 to 95 = very good program
68 to 83 = good program
42 to 67 = fair progrm
0 to 41 = poor program

VIRGULE-MARK-COUNT GRID

	EXCELLENT	VERY GOOD	GOOD	FAIR	POOR
#1					
#3					
#4					
#5					
#6					
#7					
#8					
#9					
#10					
#11					
#12					
#13					
#14					
#15					
#16					
#17					

TOTAL VIRGULE					

PARENT EVALUATION OF THE INSTRUMENTAL MUSIC PROGRAM

Place a checkmark in the box that best describes the level achieved by the instrumental music program.

1. The performance level of the band/orchestra is:

EXCELLENT	VERY GOOD	GOOD	FAIR	POOR

2. The instrumental music program provides continued training for the individual band/orchestra member at a level that is:

EXCELLENT	VERY GOOD	GOOD	FAIR	POOR

3. The scheduling for the band/orchestra rehearsals during the school day is:

EXCELLENT	VERY GOOD	GOOD	FAIR	POOR

4. The level of musicianship of the average band/orchestra member is:

EXCELLENT	VERY GOOD	GOOD	FAIR	POOR

5. The scheduling of class lessons is:

EXCELLENT	VERY GOOD	GOOD	FAIR	POOR

6. The concert schedule, i.e., the number of concerts given each year by the band/orchestra is:

EXCELLENT	VERY GOOD	GOOD	FAIR	POOR

7. The level of musical understanding of the average band/orchestra member is:

EXCELLENT	VERY GOOD	GOOD	FAIR	POOR

8. The small ensembles (chamber ensembles) recital schedule given each year by the instrumental music department is:

EXCELLENT	VERY GOOD	GOOD	FAIR	POOR

9. The quality of school instruments available to the band/orchestra is:

EXCELLENT	VERY GOOD	GOOD	FAIR	POOR

10. The level of support given the band/orchestra director and his or her program by the school administration is:

EXCELLENT	VERY GOOD	GOOD	FAIR	POOR

11. The facilities used by the band/orchestra for rehearsals are:

EXCELLENT	VERY GOOD	GOOD	FAIR	POOR

12. The budget levels given the band/orchestra by the school administration are:

EXCELLENT	VERY GOOD	GOOD	FAIR	POOR

13. The level of support given the band/orchestra director and his or her program by parents is:

EXCELLENT	VERY GOOD	GOOD	FAIR	POOR

14. The ancillary facilities for use by the band/orchestra are:

EXCELLENT	VERY GOOD	GOOD	FAIR	POOR

15. The lines of communication between the band/orchestra director and the parents are:

EXCELLENT	VERY GOOD	GOOD	FAIR	POOR

16. The regular (or periodic) methods for the band/orchestra director communication with parents are:

EXCELLENT	VERY GOOD	GOOD	FAIR	POOR

17. The conditions of the equipment being used by the band/orchestra are:

EXCELLENT	VERY GOOD	GOOD	FAIR	POOR

18. The solo recital schedule, i.e., the number of recital programs given each year by the instrumental music department is:

EXCELLENT	VERY GOOD	GOOD	FAIR	POOR

19. The quality of the equipment available for use by the band/orchestra is:

EXCELLENT	VERY GOOD	GOOD	FAIR	POOR

20. The condition of the facilities used by the band/orchestra is:

EXCELLENT	VERY GOOD	GOOD	FAIR	POOR

21. The frequency of scheduled band/orchestra rehearsals is:

EXCELLENT	VERY GOOD	GOOD	FAIR	POOR

22. The method used for giving band/orchestra report card grades is:

EXCELLENT	VERY GOOD	GOOD	FAIR	POOR

23. The type of music the band/orchestra plays for concerts is:

EXCELLENT	VERY GOOD	GOOD	FAIR	POOR

24. My child's attitude toward the band/orchestra is:

EXCELLENT	VERY GOOD	GOOD	FAIR	POOR

The space provided below may be used to comment on any aspect of the program you may wish to address.

_____

_____

_____

_____

_____

_____

_____

CRITERION MODEL #13

Evaluation of Department Chairperson

DATE: _____

   TO: <u>All Music Teachers</u>

FROM: _____

SUBJECT: <u>Evaluation of Department Chairperson</u>

Would you please complete the evaluation form contained herein and return it to me at your earliest convenience. Please do not sign your name. Your remarks should remain anonymous.

INTRODUCTION

In an attempt to better serve the needs of those involved in the music department, it is important that the effectiveness of the department chairperson as an educational leader be periodically evaluated. No one is so nearly perfect that improvement is impossible, although few are aware of their specific handicaps. As you well know, self-perception is not synonymous with perception of others. Each student, each staff member, and each parent has his or her own perception of the contacts shared with the department chairperson, and these perceptions vary greatly. It is the purpose of this evaluation tool to collect these varying perceptions so that ultimately the effectiveness of the department chairperson may be increased. Therefore, your candid observations and notations will be greatly appreciated.

Please indicate your response to each item below by entering a number in the space provided that most nearly or accurately fits in the area of the question mark. Respond to all items according to your point of view.

RATING KEY

The number given refers to the word or phrase of evaluation. Each number does not mean all the items given but one or the other where applicable.

     4 = excellent, or always, or a high degree of. . . .
     3 = good, or almost always, or a sufficient degree of. . . .
     2 = fair, or sometimes, or a fair degree of. . . .
     1 = poor, or never, or a low degree of. . . .
     U = unable to determine (please use this letter sparingly)

I. PERSONAL QUALITIES

_____ 1. Is (?) consistent in his or her actions.

_____ 2. (?) has an enthusiastic outlook.

_____ 3. Displays (?) qualities of leadership.

_____ 4. Has (?) rapport with teacher.

_____ 5. Has (?) rapport with students.

_____ 6. Has (?) rapport with parents.

_____ 7. Is (?) calm and even-tempered.

_____ 8. Possesses and exercises (?) tact and good judgment.

_____ 9. Shows (?) poise and maturity of action under most circumstances.

_____ 10. (?) uses good English, expresses him or herself clearly, and is easily understood.

_____ 11. Voice is (?) clear, pleasing, and well-modulated.

_____ 12. Possesses and displays (?) energy and vitality to meet his or her daily obligations.

_____ 13. (?) keeps abreast of professional events and shares this with all concerned.

_____ 14. Has a/an (?) knowledge of the program's needs.

_____ 15. Is (?) neat in appearance.

_____ 16. Shows a/an (?) efficiency and organizational ability.

_____ 17. Is (?) responsive to teacher's needs.

Feel free to comment on any of the above items or to focus on other "Personal Qualities" not mentioned.

_____

_____

_____

_____

_____

_____

II. CHAIRPERSON-STAFF RELATIONSHIPS

——— 1. Is (?) kind, sympathetic, and patient with staff members.

——— 2. Is (?) friendly, but not in excess.

——— 3. Has a/an (?) attitude that leads toward mutual cooperation and respect.

——— 4. (?) avoids sarcasm and embarrassment toward staff members.

——— 5. Is (?) impartial in dealing with staff members.

——— 6. (?) praises and gives favorable criticism when warranted.

——— 7. (?) invites discussion and teacher participation at departmental meetings whenever possible.

——— 8. (?) stands up for and defends staff members when problems arise.

——— 9. (?) encourages experimentation in methods and technic by staff members.

——— 10. (?) withholds expressions of anger in front of staff members.

——— 11. Is (?) responsive in meeting requests of assistance.

——— 12. Shows a (?) of interest in the activities of various musical organizations.

Feel free to comment on any of the above items or to focus on other "Chairperson-Staff Relationships" not mentioned above.

_____

_____

_____

_____

_____

_____

_____

_____

This evaluation and statements contained herein are in no way conclusive to its end. No doubt there are other things that could be included. Because of this, would you please focus on three or more areas of my strengths or weaknesses according to your perceptions and develop them below.

It is hoped this evaluation will in turn provide me with the insight in which to better serve all those involved in the music department.

Thank you for your assistance.

CRITERION MODEL #14

SURVEY on STYLES & PERIODS of COMPOSITIONS PERFORMED

The following checklists are designed to give the band/orchestra director a view of the breadth of offerings he/she makes available to the students. By keeping this record the director can view the variety and styles of compositions selected over a year's concertizing. To use these survey forms do the following:

The "Survey On. . . ." form is to be filled out for each concert and/or presentation made by the band/orchestra during the school year. Every performance, even if it uses the same materials, should be entered as a separate performance. This would also include the materials used for contests and/or festivals.

Step #1: Using the "Survey On. . . ." form, enter the titles of each composition performed at a given concert or any other public performance. Space is provided for just the key words of the title of each composition.

Step #2: Using the categorical descriptions that follow, place a checkmark in the appropriate box after the composition's title that best describes it as to "Style" and another checkmark that would indicate its "Period."

Step #3: Add up the total number of checkmarks (See Work Sheet).

Step #4: Divide that number (from Step 3) into the number of checkmarks in each category to arrive at the percent, and enter that number at the bottom of the "Survey On. . . ." form.

Step #5: Transfer these percentages to the "Composite Of. . . ." chart, entering the date of each performance and the percentages.

Step #6: Do the same thing with each concert and presentation and at the end of the year, average these percentages for a view of the year's offerings.

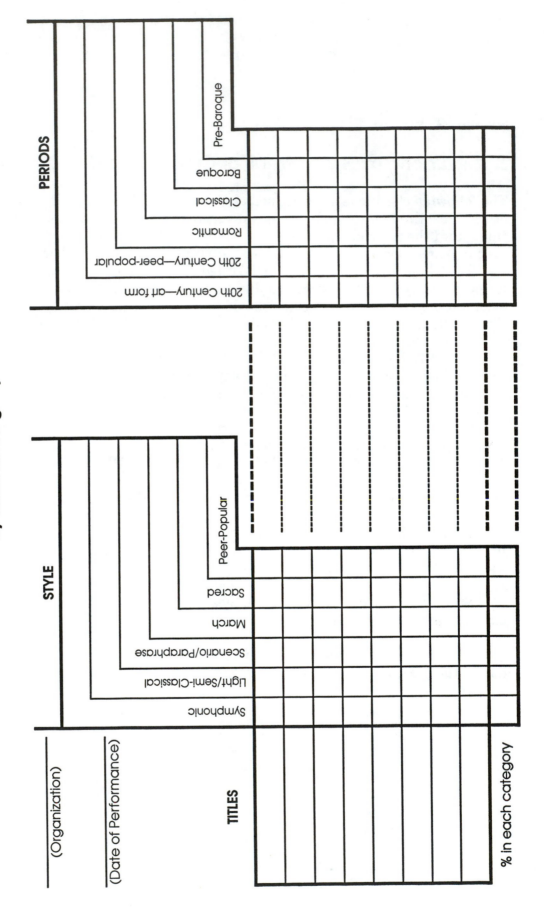

SURVEY ON:
STYLES AND PERIODS OF COMPOSITIONS PERFORMED
by instrumental groups

COMPOSITE OF SURVEY
ON STYLES AND PERIODS OF COMPOSITIONS PERFORMED

Instrumental groups _____ During school year _____

STYLE

DATES of PERFORMANCES	Symphonic	Light/Semi-Classical	Scenario/Paraphrase	March	Sacred	Peer-Popular
COMPOSITE %						

PERIODS

	20th Century—art form	20th Century—peer-popular	Romantic	Classical	Baroque	Pre-Baroque

COMPOSITE OF STYLES & PERIODS WORKSHEET

**TOTAL NUMBER OF
MARKS UNDER:**   **UNDER STYLE** _____

Symphonic   _____ — _____ " = _____%
Light/Semi-Classical   _____ — _____ " = _____%
Scenario/Paraphrase   _____ — _____ " = _____%
March   _____ — _____ " = _____%
Sacred   _____ — _____ " = _____%
Peer-Popular   _____ — _____ " = _____%

**TOTAL NUMBER OF
MARKS UNDER:**   **UNDER PERIODS** _____

20th Century—art forms   _____ — _____ " = _____%
20th Century—Peer-Popular   _____ — _____ " = _____%
Romantic   _____ — _____ " = _____%
Classical   _____ — _____ " = _____%
Baroque   _____ — _____ " = _____%
Pre-Baroque   _____ — _____ " = _____%

CATEGORICAL DESCRIPTIONS

Under Symphonic

Symphony, concerto, sonata, sonatina, rondo, suite, partita, divertimento, fugue, fantasy, impromptu, passacaglia, toccata, overture, prelude, symphonic poem, etc.

Under Light/Semi-Classical

Peer-popular works arranged in a "classical" setting may be classed here particularly if they are arranged in concert style and orchestrated like a symphonic work, i.e., not just a simple statement and restatement of the melodic idea. Also classed here would be works like concert versions of Latin-American dances like "Blue Tango" by Anderson, and traditional dances like a polka, waltz, or tarantella, if not of a purely popular nature.

Under Scenario/Paraphrase

Arrangements of folk songs, selections or excerpts from Broadway musicals, and arrangements of and renditions of patriotic works. This would also include works like "Winter Wonderland" and other seasonal works with fairly sophisticated arrangements. A fairly straight rendition of a song like "Winter Wonderland" should be classed as peer-popular.

Under March

This includes the quick-step band marches, concert marches, and processionals, if not of a symphonic nature. Items like "Procession of Nobles" and the "March" from *Aida* would be classed as symphonic.

Under Sacred

This would include such things as Christmas carols and special arrangements of hymns. If it is a composition based on themes of Palestrina or the like, it could be classed under symphonic if the arrangement is not purely a statement of themes in different instrumental timbres.

Under Peer-Popular

This includes the broad category of jazz, e.g., dixieland, swing, progressive jazz, or blues, as well as rock. It would also include any compositions written in the style of the "Big Bands" of the Dorsey, Ellington, and Miller era, settings of popular songs like "Star Dust," novelties of any kind, and patriotic songs and selections such as *Spotlight on George M. Cohan.*

Under Twentieth Century Peer-Popular

This category is for all types of popular music composed during the twentieth century or folk music with no specific symphonic setting. Where the intent is definitely symphonic, e.g., *Suite of Old American Dances*, classify it under twentieth century—art forms.

CRITERION MODEL #15

CONCERT SURVEY—AUDIENCE REACTIONS

Please complete the questions below. This is meant to be an anonymous survey so no names are being requested.

1. Was the concert too long?   YES ☐   NO ☐

2. Was there sufficient classical music on the program?
   YES ☐   NO ☐

3. Was there sufficient popular music on the program?
   YES ☐   NO ☐

4. Give the name of one composition on the program and indicate how it was enjoyed.

   Name of Composition: _____

   I enjoyed it

   A great deal ☐   Somewhat ☐

   Not very much ☐   Not at all ☐

5. If the answer to #4 was negative, why were your feelings negative?

   _____

   _____
   (use the reverse side if necessary)

6. Could you understand the announcements?
   YES ☐   NO ☐

7. If you had to rate the quality of the performance, would it be:

   Excellent ☐   Fair ☐

   Very Good ☐   Poor ☐

   Good ☐

8. Was the auditorium conducive to an enjoyable listening experience?
   YES ☐   NO ☐

181

9. Did you think the audience was:

    ☐ Attentive   ☐ Somewhat noisy

    ☐ Moderately attentive   ☐ Too noisy

10. How many concerts have you attended this year?

    at school _____,

    in the district _____,

    by professional groups outside of the school _____.

11. If you have some relationship to someone who was a part of the performance, give that relationship, i.e., father, brother, grandparent, etc.

    _____

12. Is there anything we could do to make for greater enjoyment at our future concerts?

    _____

    _____

    _____

    _____

    _____

    _____

CRITERION MODEL #16

EVALUATION OF REHEARSAL PROCEDURES

Evaluate each item in the criteria as follows:

E—if the provision or condition is made extensively
S—if the provision or condition is made to some extent
L—if the provision or condition is limited
M—if the provision or condition is missing and needed
N—if the provision or condition does not apply or is not necessarily desirable

Final outcomes, if desired, may be figured based on the procedures given in Criterion Model #1.

_____ 1. A systematic way is established for taking care of instrument cases, school books, and wraps so they do not clutter the rehearsal area.

_____ 2. There is a definite seating plan set up in a uniform manner each day before the rehearsal begins.

_____ 3. Chairs and music stands are evenly spaced with enough clearance for students to be able to handle their instruments without interference from the persons sitting side by side.

_____ 4. Daily attendance is taken in a manner that does not interfere with the rehearsal.

_____ 5. Ventilation is adjusted, heat regulated, and lights adjusted before the rehearsal begins.

_____ 6. All large percussion instruments are placed and adjusted before the rehearsal begins.

_____ 7. All special equipment such as a stereo and records, charts, metronome, etc., are placed and adjusted before the rehearsal begins.

_____ 8. The rehearsal routine is divided into a warm-up period, turning period, technical drill, playing of unfinished work, and sight reading, before concluding with familiar material.

_____ 9. Drills focus on different passages of a few numbers. These numbers are not played all the way through.

_____ 10. At each rehearsal at least one piece is played all they way through.

_____ 11. There is no unnecessary playing of instruments before, during, or after rehearsals in the halls or other rooms not designated for practicing.

_____ 12. Students are not allowed to blow each other's instruments.

_____ 13. Music stands are each adjusted so the students reading off them can see the conductor.

_____ 14. At no time are more than two students allowed to read from one music stand.

_____ 15. While playing, students maintain good posture and hold instruments properly (bells parallel with the floor for brasses, clarinets at the right angle, flutes held up, etc.)

_____ 16. Instruments are put away and folders closed only after the director gives permission.

_____ 17. The music room and accompanying rooms are kept in orderly fashion at all times, with all music and instruments in their designated places.

_____ 18. Anyone on the podium (director, student, or guest) is given the group's complete attention.

_____ 19. When the director is on the podium, instruments are at the position of attention.

_____ 20. When the director is off the podium, instruments are in rest position.

_____ 21. Only questions dealing with music being played are honored during the rehearsal. All other questions and problems that arise are dealt with after the rehearsal has concluded.

_____ 22. No student is allowed to leave the rehearsal to get reeds, oil, tighten screws, etc. They may leave only in cases of emergencies like illness or because of prior permission.

_____ 23. When not playing, percussionists either stand behind their equipment or have chairs on which to sit.

_____ 24. Second chair players know that they are responsible for music—turning pages, care, etc.

_____ 25. The concert folders are kept in order by the students using them.

_____ 26. The concert folders are systematically kept in order as follows: books at the back-right with concert-size in front, octavo and march-size on the left.

_____ 27. If there is a large number of similar-sized pieces in the folder, they are placed in alphabetical order.

_____ 28. Music folders are in good condition.

_____ 29. All music is signed out before it is taken home for practice.

_____ 30. Students coming into the senior high organization, or those transferring from other schools, are given an orientation program of some sort.

_____ 31. A handbook of information is available for students and parents which explains standard operating procedures.

_____ 32. Student officers are elected and/or appointed to assist the director.

_____ 33. Student officers know what their duties are through the handbook or other such means of permanent information.

_____ 34. There is a policy strictly against using xerox copies of copyrighted music.

CRITERION MODEL #17

EVALUATING CONDUCTORIAL DIRECTIVES

Evaluate the following criteria* with the use of these ratings:

> A—Always
> B—Almost always
> C—Most of the time
> D—Some of the time
> F—Almost never or not very often

_____ 1. The group is trained so that everyone stops when signaled to do so and remains silent.

_____ 2. Before interrupting the playing, the conductor is sure of what he is going to say.

_____ 3. When the group is stopped, comments are begun without hesitation.

_____ 4. Comments are formulated in terms of clearly defined technical advice.

_____ 5. Repetitions of a section or portions of a composition are made after giving the group good reasons, unless things have gone wrong to the extent that the necessity for repeating is obvious.

_____ 6. When remarks are to be addressed to one section or individual, the instruments are first identified, then the passage in question, then an explanation is given why the passage was not satisfactory.

_____ 7. Discussion of extended solo passages take place at times other than during full rehearsals.

_____ 8. Musical details are discussed only after the players have turned to the appropriate page and know exactly what is being talked about.

_____ 9. Once a passage is begun, work is continued until some improvement is noticed, unless the players are not capable of coping with a particular problem because of technical limitations.

*Max Rudolf, "Rehearsal Techniques." _The Conductor's Art_, edited by Carl Bamberger. New York: McGraw-Hill Book Co., 1965, 281.

_____ 10. When a number of measures have to be counted before or after a rehearsal number or letter, the students are given specific directions as to where to begin counting and how far to count.

_____ 11. After the proper announcement, playing is resumed as soon as is practicable and without lingering.

_____ 12. Spoken comments while the musicians are playing are used sparingly by the conductor.

CRITERION MODEL #18

CONDUCTING CRITIQUE SHEET

NAME _____ DATE _____

COMPOSITION _____

RIGHT HAND

#1 (R.H.)		excellent	very good	good	fair	poor
PREPARATORY	**speed**	☐	☐	☐	☐	☐
BEAT	**style**	☐	☐	☐	☐	☐
	dynamics	☐	☐	☐	☐	☐

☐ - eyes were on the score at the time of the preparatory beat
☐ - tempo was not pre-established in the mind
☐ - did not breathe with the preparatory beat
☐ - breath was not in character of the music

#2 (R.H.)
FUNDAMENTAL
GESTURE

☐ - eyes were on the score at the time of the fundamental gesture
☐ - rebound of the first beat or fundamental gesture was too large
the ictus of the fundamental gesture was:
☐ - good ☐ - not clear ☐ - too heavy
☐ - indefinite ☐ - out of the sight of the players

#3 (R.H.)
FIRST BEATS

☐ - clear ☐ - not clear ☐ - not precise
☐ - too stiff ☐ - too limpid ☐ - too florid
☐ - constantly too large

#4 (R.H.)
TYPES OF GESTURES
USED

☐ - legato ☐ - staccato ☐ - tenuto
☐ - syncopation ☐ - dead
☐ - all the same ☐ - very little change

#5 (R.H.)
FOCUS OF THE
BATON

☐ - beat focused at the tip of the baton
☐ - beat focused at the tip of the baton most of the time
☐ - beat focused at the tip of the baton sometimes
☐ - beat was not focused at the tip of the baton
☐ - beat was focused on the hand
☐ - beat was focused on _____

#6 (R.H.) RELEASES & CUT-OFFS	☐ - good ☐ - not clear ☐ - too heavy	☐ - awkward ☐ - not in character ☐ - none given

#7 (R.H.) DYNAMICS	☐ - changes were given - good ☐ - too much the same ☐ - all the same—no changes	☐ - very good ☐ - tends only towards *mf*

#8 (R.H.) ATTACK POINTS	☐ - good ☐ - out of sight	☐ - not clear ☐ - too heavy

#9 (R.H.) STYLE	☐ - good ☐ - degrees of legato and staccato not differentiated ☐ - staccato too heavy	☐ - made no changes ☐ - legato too heavy

#10 (R.H.) CUING	☐ - good ☐ - not soon enough at times ☐ - not clear to whom or which section ☐ - too forcefully given ☐ - none given	☐ - good but awkward

#11 (L.H.) TIME BEATING	☐ - right amount of use ☐ - far too much use ☐ - regularly beats only part of the measure	☐ - too much use of ☐ - used all the time

#12 (L.H.) CUING	☐ - good ☐ - not soon enough at times ☐ - generally too late for entrances ☐ - not clear to whom or which section ☐ - too forcefully given	☐ - awkward ☐ - none given

#13 (L.H.) DYNAMICS	☐ - good-clear ☐ - give no apparent indications ☐ - indications were not successful	☐ - awkward ☐ - none given

#14 (L.H.) STYLE	☐ - good ☐ - not in character of music ☐ - not clear	☐ - awkward ☐ - too heavy ☐ - none given

#15—POSITION OF THE LEFT HAND WHEN NOT IN USE

	☐ - good ☐ - not acceptable ☐ - unable to tell because the hand was used constantly	☐ - awkward

CRITERION MODEL #19

REHEARSAL PROCEDURES MONITORING

PLACE A CHECKMARK IN A BOX EACH TIME THE ITEM OCCURS

Percent of total # of checkmarks ⟶

1. tutti playing

   ☐ ☐ ☐ ☐ ☐ ☐ ☐ ☐ ☐ ☐ ☐ ☐ ☐ ☐ ☐
   ☐ ☐ ☐ ☐ ☐ ☐ ☐ ☐ ☐ ☐ ☐ ☐ ☐ ☐ ☐
   ☐ ☐ ☐ ☐ ☐ ☐ ☐ ☐ ☐ ☐ ☐ ☐ ☐ ☐ ☐   ____

2. sectional playing

   ☐ ☐ ☐ ☐ ☐ ☐ ☐ ☐ ☐ ☐ ☐ ☐ ☐ ☐ ☐   ____

3. individual playing

   ☐ ☐ ☐ ☐ ☐ ☐ ☐ ☐ ☐ ☐ ☐ ☐ ☐ ☐ ☐   ____

4. divided sectional playing

   ☐ ☐ ☐ ☐ ☐ ☐ ☐ ☐ ☐ ☐ ☐ ☐ ☐ ☐ ☐   ____

5. isolated small group playing

   ☐ ☐ ☐ ☐ ☐ ☐ ☐ ☐ ☐ ☐ ☐ ☐ ☐ ☐ ☐   ____

6. repetitions of portions of a composition

   ☐ ☐ ☐ ☐ ☐ ☐ ☐ ☐ ☐ ☐ ☐ ☐ ☐ ☐ ☐   ____

7. verbal directions to musicians

   ☐ ☐ ☐ ☐ ☐ ☐ ☐ ☐ ☐ ☐ ☐ ☐ ☐ ☐ ☐
   ☐ ☐ ☐ ☐ ☐ ☐ ☐ ☐ ☐ ☐ ☐ ☐ ☐ ☐ ☐   ____

8. non-verbal directions via conductoral technic

   ☐ ☐ ☐ ☐ ☐ ☐ ☐ ☐ ☐ ☐ ☐ ☐ ☐ ☐ ☐
   ☐ ☐ ☐ ☐ ☐ ☐ ☐ ☐ ☐ ☐ ☐ ☐ ☐ ☐ ☐   ____

9. questions for clarification by musicians

   ☐ ☐ ☐ ☐ ☐ ☐ ☐ ☐ ☐ ☐ ☐ ☐ ☐ ☐ ☐   ____

total number of check marks were ____

CRITERION MODEL #20

ENSEMBLE TECHNIQUES MONITORING
General Techniques

PLACE A CHECKMARK IN A BOX EACH TIME THE ITEM IS DISCUSSED

Percent of total # of checkmarks ⟶

1. Tone

□ □ □ □ □ □ □ □ □ □ □ □ □ □ □ □ ____

2. Intonation

□ □ □ □ □ □ □ □ □ □ □ □ □ □ □ □ ____

3. Balance

□ □ □ □ □ □ □ □ □ □ □ □ □ □ □ □ ____

4. Blend

□ □ □ □ □ □ □ □ □ □ □ □ □ □ □ □ ____

5. Precision

□ □ □ □ □ □ □ □ □ □ □ □ □ □ □ □ ____

6. Rhythm

□ □ □ □ □ □ □ □ □ □ □ □ □ □ □ □ ____

7. Style

□ □ □ □ □ □ □ □ □ □ □ □ □ □ □ □ ____

8. Tempo

□ □ □ □ □ □ □ □ □ □ □ □ □ □ □ □ ____

9. Phrasing

□ □ □ □ □ □ □ □ □ □ □ □ □ □ □ □ ____

10. Interpretation

□ □ □ □ □ □ □ □ □ □ □ □ □ □ □ □ ____

11. Dynamics

□ □ □ □ □ □ □ □ □ □ □ □ □ □ □ □ ____

total number of check marks is _____

191

CRITERION MODEL #21

EVALUATING THE QUALITY OF A CLARINET

Grade each item in this criteria as A, B, C, D, or F. To receive an A (which is defined as "excellent"), the provision as stated is made to the fullest extent, adheres to the best possible standard, does not exceed necessary requirements, or is not in excess. In some cases, excess gadgets are not desirable and lead to complications. In this area, an A will not be given. In many areas the provision is cut and dry—either it has or does not have what is listed. In this case, it is either A or F.

To determine the final results, add up the letters and divide by the total number of items in the criteria. Letter values are as follows: $A = 4, B = 3, C = 2, D = 1, F = 0$. The final values would be converted as follows:

$$3.3 \text{ to } 4.0 = \text{Excellent}$$
$$2.5 \text{ to } 3.2 = \text{Very good}$$
$$1.7 \text{ to } 2.4 = \text{Good}$$
$$0.9 \text{ to } 1.6 = \text{Fair}$$
$$0.0 \text{ to } 0.8 = \text{Poor}$$

BODY

_____ 1. Wood is dense, well-seasoned, first grade Mozambique Grendilla.

_____ 2. The bore is highly polished, has smooth surfaces, is free from rough spots and imperfections.

_____ 3. Tone holes are raised and integral with the body except the thumb hole and register tube.

KEY MECHANISM

_____ 4. Fingering system is full Boehm with seventeen keys and six rings.

_____ 5. Key tension is adjusted for maximum speed and evenness of touch.

_____ 6. Keys and tone holes are constructed to fit comfortably under the fingers. (Tone holes are of necessity not in line.)

KEY CONSTRUCTION

_____ 7. Keys are hand-carved, hard-hammered virgin nickel-silver.

_____ 8. Keys are highly polished to a natural finish, free of tool marks and other imperfections.

_____ 9. Keys have reinforced arms and cups.

_____ 10. Keys and posts are precision fitted to allow only a minute horizontal movement.

_____ 11. Tone rings are centered perfectly around tone holes.

_____ 12. Bridge keys have protectors.

_____ 13. A heavy duty "crowfoot" is constructed on the C/F and the B/E key.

_____ 14. There is a male-female linkage between left hand E/B and C♯/F♯ keys.

_____ 15. A long hinge is provided through the throat G♯ key.

_____ 16. There is a long bearing surface on all key rods.

_____ 17. There are separate post mountings for side trill keys.

_____ 18. Individual post mountings are provided for:
   (a) throat G♯ and A key
   (b) C♯/G♯ keys
   (c) each of the long levers of the upper joint
   (d) the E/B and F♯/C♯ levers of the lower joint

CONSTRUCTION OF FITTINGS

_____ 19. Pivot and hinge screws are of high carbon stainless steel.

_____ 20. Pivot and hinge screws are carefully constructed so screwdriver slots are in the center of the screw head.

_____ 21. Finest blue-steel springs are used throughout.

_____ 22. Screw-in type posts are provided throughout.

FITTINGS

_____ 23. Tenon rings are provided on the upper end of the lower joint and both ends of the barrel.

_____ 24. The thumb rest is contoured.

_____ 25. The thumb rest is located at the balancing point.

ADJUSTMENTS

_____ 26. There are a minimum number of set screws, and those that are provided are workable.

_____ 27. Adjustable center screw is provided on the throat G♯ key.

_____ 28. There are a limited number of locking devices (post and pivot screws).

PADS AND CORKS

_____ 29. Pads are of resilient woven felt, covered with double thickness, high quality fish skin.

_____ 30. Cork is top grade, smooth, and ungrained.

_____ 31. Cork bumpers are provided on:

(a) upper side of the register key

(b) upper side of the C♯/G♯ key

(c) upper side of the E♭/G♯ key

(d) upper side of the throat G♯ key

(e) upper side of the E♭/B♭ key

(f) between the throat G♯ and A key

(g) both sides of the bridge key

(h) thumb rest

_____ 32. Tenon corks are fitted to exact length of tenon cork receivers and glued in an overlapping manner.

MOUTHPIECES & ACCESSORIES

_____ 33. The mouthpiece is constructed of drilled rod rubber.

_____ 34. All surfaces are smooth and free of scratches.

_____ 35. The mouthpiece has a medium lay, accurately faced, and with inside diameter matching the bore of the clarinet.

_____ 36. The mouthpiece is numbered as to the lay proportions.

_____ 37. The mouthpiece is stamped with the manufacturer's name.

_____ 38. A ligature placement ring is imprinted into the mouthpiece.

_____ 39. The ligature is of one piece construction fitted with two wing screws.

_____ 40. The ligature is of proper size to fit standard mouthpieces and conforms to the shape of the reed and mouthpiece.

_____ 41. The ligature screws are made from one piece construction.

_____ 42. The nuts of the ligature are soldered securely to the ligature.

_____ 43. The mouthpiece cap fits over the reed and mouthpiece securely and has an opening in the top for ventilation.

CASE

_____ 44. The box is of solid construction.

_____ 45. The outside material is durable and washable.

_____ 46. The case sits level without rocking.

_____ 47. The interior trays are lined with soft, resilient plush or mohair.

_____ 48. The trays are fitted to the contours of the instrument.

_____ 49. The trays do not allow parts to touch each other.

_____ 50. A separate tray is provided for each of the six sections of the instrument.

_____ 51. Sufficient space is provided for extra reeds, swab, cork grease, and screw driver.

_____ 52. Latches on the case are large and durable.

_____ 53. The case will stay open when assembling the instrument.

_____ 54. The case handles are mounted securely and are of solid construction.

MUSICAL PROPERTIES

_____ 55. The instrument has a characteristic clarinet tone.

_____ 56. All notes throughout all registers are even in quality.

_____ 57. Keys are adjusted to the proper height so notes are neither sharp, flat, nor fuzzy sounding.

_____ 58. There is an evenness of scale throughout.

_____ 59. All scales are easily played in tune.

_____ 60. The instrument is tuned easily to A-440.

MANUFACTURER'S REPUTATION

_____ 61. The company has a reputation for fine clarinets.

_____ 62. The company has the ability to control the consistent quality of their instruments.

_____ 63. The company has a reputation of backing up the quality of their merchandise.

_____ 64. There is a good warrantee or guarantee with each instrument.

Part 3

Appendixes

CURRICULUM OUTLINE

I. LEVEL OF LEARNING

5th grade

II. COURSE DESCRIPTION

Beginning instrumental lessons

III. GENERAL OBJECTIVES

The teaching of fundamentals of music as applied to the playing of a musical instrument

IV. UNIT TOPICS

1—Instrumental techniques and solo playing

2—Musicianship training

3—Ensemble rehearsal

V. TIME ALLOCATIONS

One forty-minute period for each unit

VI. UNIT TOPIC #1

Instrumental techniques and solo playing

A. Importance

Through this topic, the student learns the skills necessary for perfor mance on his/her instrument. The student is guided through various materials so he/she can some day take part and be a contributing member of the school band and/or orchestra.

B. Overview of the Unit

All like instruments meet in a small group of not more than six students.

C. General Objectives

The students are introduced to the fundamentals of tone production, rhythmic manipulation, and technic as applied to their chosen instrument. The teacher is able to solve individual problems that might arise that are characteristic of the instruments grouped into each class.

D. Performance Objectives

1. Perform in class the materials assigned in the lesson book.
2. Match tones with a tuning device.
3. Perform with the aid of a metronome.

E. Behavioral Objectives

1. Know the basic parts of the instrument and be able to describe their function.
2. Be able to form a correct embouchure on the wind instruments, properly hold the instrument, form a good hand position on the strings, and form the proper grip on the drum sticks.
3. Assemble the instrument properly.
4. Show proper care of the instrument.
5. Demonstrate such playing procedures as starting the tone, sustaining the tone, and stopping the tone.
6. Be able to properly finger written notes within musical scores.
7. Be able to properly spell letter names of notes rhythmically accurate.
8. Be able to clap and count rhythms encountered in the instruction book.
9. Use proper articulation as called for in the printed score.
10. Correlate written rhythmic figures with the tapping of the foot.
11. Demonstrate a playing knowledge of. . . .
    a. Rhythm—whole, half, quarter, eighth, dotted-quarter and eighth combinations and syncopation.
    b. Meter signatures of 4/4, 3/4, and 2/4.
    c. Key signatures of C, F, and G (where applicable)—for percussion, know the following rudiments: (1) five, seven, and nine stroke roll, (2) flam
    d. Musical terms such as: slur, tie, anacrusis, D.C. al Fine, forte and piano, staccato, legato, mezzo-forte, mezzo-piano, crescendo, diminuendo, allegro, and andante.

F. Motivating Activities

1. Upon acquisition of the necessary technic, students will begin work on the solos in *Breeze Easy Recital Pieces*.
2. Perform in solo recitals and school programs.
3. Perform with the band and/or orchestra—an all-city band/orchestra will be organized for the outstanding instrumentalists.
4. Parents will be sent letters informing them of the problems being

encountered by the beginning instrumentalists, e.g., "Letter to Parent" by M. Zimmer, *The Instrumentalist*, XXVII, 8, (March, 1973), 14.

G. Culminating Activities

1. Performances of several solos from the *Breeze Easy Recital Pieces*.
2. Tape recordings of solos for future reference and evaluation.

H. Evaluative Activities

1. Check on weekly practice reports.
2. Record weekly grades of excellent, good, or fair in the lesson book, or issue stickers for accurate performance.
3. Issue quarterly report cards.
4. Test on performance ability through the *Watkins-Farnum Performance Scale*.

I. Resources

1. Fred Weber, *First Division Band Method, Book I*. Belwin-Mills, Inc., Melville, N.Y.
2. John Kinyon, *Breeze Easy Recital Pieces*. M. Witmark, 488 Madison Ave., N.Y.
3. Drs. John G. Watkins and Stephen E. Farnum, *Watkins-Farnum Performance Scale*. Hal Leonard, Inc., Winona, Minn.

VI. UNIT TOPIC #2 MUSICIANSHIP TRAINING (5th grade)

A. Importance

Only through the knowledge of such items as care of the instrument, position of the body and hands in relation to the instrument, methods of practicing, and correct breathing or bowing can instrumental study be truly successful.

B. Overview of the Unit

Instruments of the same family meet together—all woodwinds, all brass, all strings, all percussion.

C. General Objectives

1. The eliminating of problems before they arise.
2. The gaining of an understanding of the characteristics and idiosyncrasies of the instruments.
3. Correlation of musical literature with other fields of knowledge.

D. Specific Objectives

    1. Discussion of:

        a. Care of the instruments.

        b. Hand positions are related to the playing of the instruments.

        c. Methods of learning the instrumental materials given in the technic class, and applying good methods of study and practice during home practice periods are stressed.

        d. Proper breathing/bowing methods necessary for good tone production are described and exercised.

    2. Knowledge of note-finger correlation.

    3. Historical or musical backgrounds and/or technic of the solos being studied.

    4. Understanding of how sound is created—scientifically.

E. Motivating Activities

Performance of solos for the class and taping them for future references. Also, the showing of films as listed below.

F. Developmental Activities

Performance of notated music on their instruments and the playing of tunes recognizable to the students as well as their parents.

G. Culminating Activities

Presenting papers on the backgrounds of the solos studied and performed, as well as doing research papers on subjects that come up in class.

H. Evaluative Activities

Testing on the knowledge of the material covered under letter "D"— SPECIFIC OBJECTIVES

I. Resources

Note Speller by Fred Weber. Belwin Mills, Inc.

Filmstrips: "An Introduction to the (Flute, Clarinet, etc.)"

"Scholastic Production" (Prentice-Hall)

"Noise and Musical Notes"—EAV

"Band Instrument Care"—Encyclopedia Britannica

VI. UNIT TOPIC #3 ENSEMBLE REHEARSAL (5th grade)

A. Importance

Instruction in routines to be used later when members are accepted into the band and orchestra. Further acquisition of knowledge necessary for participating in a mixed group of players.

B. Overview of Unit

This is a pre-band/orchestra instruction for all instrumentalists of the same proficiency level.

C. General Objectives

Acquisition of knowledge to make the student worthy and capable of band and orchestra participation.

D. Specific Objectives

1. Understanding general rules used during rehearsals
2. Understanding the terminology used in large ensemble literature
3. Discussion of information necessary to pass the first-year test
4. Study of items that constitute errors in performance and how they can be correlated including:
   a. pitch errors
   b. time errors (rhythm)
   c. changes of time errors
   d. expression errors
   e. slur errors
   f. rests
   g. fermata and other pauses
   h. repeats
5. Instruction in the history of the instruments

E. Motivating Activities

With successful completion of this phase of instruction, the student will be qualified to begin playing in the school band or orchestra.

F. Developmental Activities

The students develop an understanding of the problems involved in a total band and orchestra performance; that individuals must learn to accept criticism based on the needs for better playing habits on the part of all involved in the organization.

G. Culminating Activities

Performance of elementary band and orchestra materials in keeping with technical abilities.

H. Evaluative Activities

Written tests on materials studied in class. Grading of papers turned in on various aspects of music

I. Resources

Standard band and orchestra literature of a very easy degree of difficulty:

"Early Musical Instruments" by J. Weston Walch Pub., Portland, Maine (11″ by 14″ posters with commentaries).

Filmstrip: "Once Upon a Sound"—Scott Graphics, Inc.

Musical Books for Young People—Lerner Pub. Co.

C.V.D.L. EQUALIZATION CHARTS

C.V.D.L. (Composite Values of DoD vs. LoPP)

For system-wide evaluation:

Chart I	. . . . .for schools with grades K through 5
Chart II	. . . . .for schools with grades K through 6
Chart III	. . . . .for schools with grades K through 8
Chart IV	. . . . .for schools with grades 6 through 8
Chart V	. . . . .for junior high schools
Chart VI	. . . . .for senior high schools

For grades for individual student soloists:

For 5th grades	. . . . .Chart IA
For 6th grades	. . . . .Chart IIa
For 7th grades	. . . . .Chart III if standard is F = 64
For 7th grades	. . . . .Chart IIIa if standard is F = 74
For 8th grades	. . . . .Chart IV if standard is F = 64
For 8th grades	. . . . .Chart IVa if standard is F = 74
For 9th grades	. . . . .Chart V if standard is F = 64
For 9th grades	. . . . .Chart Va if standard is F = 74
For 10th grades	. . . . .Chart V
For 11th grades	. . . . .Chart VI
For 12th grades	. . . . .Chart VI

CORRELATION GUIDE

For difficulty vs. grade vs. class for various means of classifying the degree of technical and musical difficulty of a musical composition.

VERY EASY		= VE	= Grade I	= Class E	= DoD-1
EASY		= E	= Grade II	= Class D	= DoD-2
MEDIUM EASY		= ME	= Grade III	= Class C	= DoD-3
MEDIUM DIFFICULT	= MD	= Grade IV	= Class B	= DoD-4
DIFFICULT		= D	= Grade V	= Class A	= DoD-5
VERY DIFFICULT		= VD	= Grade VI	= Class AA	= DoD-6

EQUALIZATION CHART I

GiS-5 − 1 A+ = 100 with F = 64

	DoD	6	5	4	3	2	1
L E V E L O F P E R F O R M A N C E P R O F I C I E N C Y	A+	115	114	112	109	105	100
	A	109	108	107	105	101	97
	A−	103	102	102	100	97	94
	B+	96	96	97	95	93	91
	B	89	90	92	90	89	88
	B−	82	84	86	86	85	85
	C+	75	78	80	80	81	82
	C	68	72	74	75	77	79
	C−	61	66	68	70	73	76
	D+	54	59	62	65	69	73
	D	47	52	56	60	65	69
	D−	40	45	50	55	60	65
	F	33	38	44	50	55	61

EQUALIZATION CHART Ia

GiS-5 − 1 A+ = 100 with F = 74

DoD	6	5	4	3	2	1
A+	115	114	112	109	105	100
A	109	109	108	105	102	98
A−	103	104	104	101	99	96
B+	97	99	100	97	96	94
B	91	94	95	93	93	92
B−	85	89	90	89	90	90
C	79	84	85	85	87	88
C	73	79	80	81	84	86
C−	67	73	75	77	81	84
D+	62	67	70	73	78	81
D	55	62	65	69	74	78
D−	49	55	60	65	70	75
F	43	49	55	60	66	72

(LEVEL OF PERFORMANCE PROFICIENCY)

EQUALIZATION CHART II

GiS-6 − 2 A+ = 100 with F = 64

DoD	6	5	4	3	2	1
A+	114	112	109	105	100	95
A	108	107	105	101	97	92
A−	102	102	100	97	94	89
B+	96	97	95	93	91	86
B	90	92	90	89	88	83
B−	84	86	85	85	85	80
C+	78	80	80	81	82	77
C	72	74	75	77	79	74
C−	66	68	70	73	76	71
D+	59	62	65	69	73	68
D	52	56	60	65	69	64
D−	45	50	55	60	65	60
F	38	44	50	55	61	56

LEVEL OF PERFORMANCE PROFICIENCY

EQUALIZATION CHART IIa

GiS-6 − 2 A+ = 100 with F = 74

	DoD	6	5	4	3	2	1
L E V E L O F P E R F O R M A N C E P R O F I C I E N C Y	A+	114	112	109	105	100	95
	A	109	108	105	102	98	93
	A−	104	104	101	99	96	91
	B+	99	100	97	96	94	89
	B	94	95	93	93	92	87
	B−	89	90	89	90	90	85
	C+	84	85	85	87	88	83
	C	79	80	81	84	86	81
	C−	73	75	77	81	84	79
	D+	67	70	73	78	81	76
	D	62	65	69	74	78	73
	D−	55	60	65	70	75	70
	F	49	55	60	66	72	61

EQUALIZATION CHART III

GiS-7 − 3 A+ = 100 with F = 64

DoD	6	5	4	3	2	1
A+	112	109	105	100	95	90
A	107	105	101	97	92	87
A−	102	100	97	94	89	84
B+	97	95	93	91	86	81
B	92	90	89	88	83	78
B−	86	85	85	85	80	75
C+	80	80	81	82	77	72
C	74	75	77	79	74	69
C−	68	70	73	76	71	66
D+	62	65	69	73	68	63
D	56	60	65	69	64	59
D−	50	55	60	65	60	55
F	44	50	55	61	56	51

LEVEL OF PERFORMANCE PROFICIENCY

EQUALIZATION CHART IIIa

GiS-7 − 3 A+ = 100 with F = 74

	DoD	6	5	4	3	2	1
L E V E L O F P E R F O R M A N C E P R O F I C I E N C Y	A+	112	109	105	100	95	90
	A	108	105	102	98	93	88
	A−	104	101	99	96	91	86
	B+	100	97	96	94	89	84
	B	95	93	93	92	87	82
	B−	90	89	90	90	85	80
	C+	85	85	87	88	83	78
	C	80	81	84	86	81	76
	C−	75	77	81	84	79	74
	D+	70	73	78	81	76	71
	D	65	69	77	78	73	68
	D−	60	65	70	75	70	65
	F	55	60	66	72	61	56

EQUALIZATION CHART IV

GiS-8 − 4 A+ = 100 with F = 64

DoD	6	5	4	3	2	1
A+	109	105	100	95	90	85
A	105	101	97	92	87	82
A−	100	97	94	89	84	79
B+	95	93	91	86	81	76
B	90	89	88	83	78	73
B−	85	85	85	80	75	70
C+	80	81	82	77	72	67
C	75	77	79	74	69	64
C−	70	73	76	71	66	61
D+	65	69	73	68	63	58
D	60	65	69	64	59	54
D−	55	60	65	60	55	50
F	50	55	61	56	51	46

LEVEL OF PERFORMANCE PROFICIENCY

EQUALIZATION CHART IVa

GiS-8 − 4 A+ = 100 with F = 74

	DoD	6	5	4	3	2	1
L **E** **V** **E** **L** **O** **F** **P** **E** **R** **F** **O** **R** **M** **A** **N** **C** **E** **P** **R** **O** **F** **I** **C** **I** **E** **N** **C** **Y**	A+	110	105	100	95	90	85
	A	106	102	98	93	88	83
	A−	102	99	96	91	86	81
	B+	98	96	94	89	84	79
	B	94	93	92	87	82	77
	B−	90	90	90	85	80	75
	C+	86	87	88	83	78	73
	C	82	84	86	81	76	71
	C−	78	81	84	79	74	69
	D+	74	78	81	76	71	66
	D	70	74	78	73	68	63
	D−	65	70	75	70	65	60
	F	60	66	72	67	62	57

EQUALIZATION CHART V

GiS-9 and -10 − 5 A+ = 100 with F = 64

DoD	6	5	4	3	2	1
A+	105	100	95	90	85	80
A	101	97	92	87	82	77
A−	97	94	89	84	79	74
B+	93	91	86	81	76	71
B	89	88	83	78	73	68
B−	85	85	80	75	70	65
C+	81	82	77	72	67	62
C	77	79	74	69	64	59
C−	73	76	71	66	61	56
D+	69	73	68	63	58	53
D	65	69	64	59	54	49
D−	60	65	60	55	50	45
F	55	61	56	51	46	41

LEVEL OF PERFORMANCE PROFICIENCY

EQUALIZATION CHART Va

GiS-9 and -10 − 5 A+ = 100 with F = 74

	DoD	6	5	4	3	2	1
L E V E L O F P E R F O R M A N C E P R O F I C I E N C Y	A+	105	100	95	90	85	90
	A	102	98	93	88	83	78
	A−	99	96	91	86	81	76
	B+	96	94	89	84	79	74
	B	93	92	87	82	77	72
	B−	90	90	85	80	75	70
	C+	87	88	83	78	73	68
	C	84	86	81	76	71	66
	C−	81	84	79	74	69	64
	D+	78	81	76	71	66	61
	D	74	78	73	68	63	58
	D−	70	75	70	65	60	55
	F	66	72	67	62	57	52

EQUALIZATION CHART VI

GiS-11 and -12 − 6 A+ = 100 with F = 64

DoD	6	5	4	3	2	1
A+	100	95	90	85	80	75
A	97	92	87	82	77	72
A−	94	89	84	79	74	69
B+	91	86	81	76	71	66
B	88	83	78	73	68	63
B−	85	80	75	70	65	60
C+	82	77	72	67	62	57
C	79	74	69	64	59	54
C−	76	71	66	61	56	51
D+	73	68	63	58	53	48
D	69	64	59	54	49	44
D−	65	60	55	50	45	40
F	61	56	51	46	41	36

LEVEL OF PERFORMANCE PROFICIENCY

Index